The Logbook of the Captain's Clerk

Adventures in the China Seas

U.S.S. Saratoga

Courtesy Special Collections Division, The Nimitz Library, United States Naval Academy, Annapolis, Maryland

The Lakeside Classics

THE LOGBOOK OF THE CAPTAIN'S CLERK

Adventures in the China Seas

By
John S. Sewall

EDITED BY
ARTHUR POWER DUDDEN

The Lakeside Press

R.R. DONNELLEY & SONS COMPANY

CHICAGO

December, 1995

THIS YEAR, our Lakeside Classic describes the American expeditions of the mid-nineteenth century that culminated in the establishment of diplomatic and trade relations with Japan.

Commodore Matthew Calbraith Perry, U.S.N., accepted the difficult task of opening Japan to the West. Where others had tried and failed, Perry succeeded through a combination of meticulous planning, a show of force, and excellent diplomatic skills. With the Treaty of Kanagawa, Perry set in motion the process whereby Western ideas, commerce, and trade eventually penetrated Japan.

The reality of this accomplishment was, however, more complicated and Perry's success less certain than a simplified history might imply. Our book, *The Logbook of the Captain's Clerk, Adventures in the China Seas*, is an eyewitness account. John S. Sewall, our author, relates the voyages of the U.S.S. *Saratoga*, a warship that set out from the United States on a routine assignment to the Far East and ended up as part of Perry's American Squadron.

The subject of this book represents something of a departure for the Lakeside Classics. For many years, we have published first-person accounts that emphasized the American West. *Logbook* signals a new editorial "horizon" for the Classics. Much as our company is engaged in entering new global markets, the Lakeside Classics series now expands its outlook to offer a more international perspective. For the next few years, we plan to focus on narratives about Americans who traveled and explored the world beyond our continental borders.

* * * *

With this volume, we say farewell to Frank Hoell, who directed the Lakeside Classics for more than sixteen years. Frank not only discovered unusual and interesting narratives, he also enhanced the reputation of the Classics. We thank him for his fine work and for giving our readers so many hours of pleasurable reading.

Arthur Power Dudden, Ph.D., the Katharine E. McBride Professor in History, Fairbank Professor Emeritus in the Humanities, and Professor of History Emeritus at Bryn Mawr College, served as historical editor for this volume. You'll find his Historical Introduction, Editor's Epilogue, and footnotes provide excellent details and an important context for the events covered in the *Logbook.*

Many of the lithographs in this book were selected from *The Expedition of an American Squadron to the China Seas and Japan*, a three-volume account of Perry's Japan voyages published in 1856. Our thanks to the University of Chicago Library, which allowed us to use these volumes for text and illustration research.

The new horizons explored in this volume also

include state-of-the-art digital processes used to create and manufacture this book. For the first time, we used a sophisticated composition technology to set type and compose pages–the same technology that enables our customers to access and manipulate vast amounts of data and then output that information in a range of print and digital media.

We electronically transmitted text and illustrations between our Database Technology Services in Willowbrook, Illinois, and our book manufacturing facility in Crawfordsville, Indiana. Maps, digitally drawn and proofed, were also transmitted electronically. Cartographers and historians at GeoSystems created these maps. GeoSystems is a former subsidiary of R.R. Donnelley and now a company in which we maintain an ownership position and with which we work closely.

Our Crawfordsville Book Manufacturing Division scanned and proofed illustrations using digital technologies. Database Technology Services received high-resolution scans electronically from Crawfordsville, combined images with text and captions, used sophisticated software to prepare the pages for plate imaging, and electronically transmitted finished pages back to Crawfordsville. In another first for the Lakeside Classics, Crawfordsville also used state-of-the-art computer-to-plate technology to transform electronic pages directly into press-ready plates.

Digital technology also enabled us to reinstate an

earlier custom of the Lakeside Classics—that of sending a personalized card along with the volume.

* * * *

In many previous Lakeside Classics, we reviewed the past year in detail, providing extensive information on our business performance. This year we wish to put our performance in a larger context, discussing the strengths behind our strategic plans.

To start with an obvious but important point, the world in which R.R. Donnelley operates is changing rapidly. We find that digital technologies—computer programs and applications, entertaining and educational CD-ROMs, the on-line services like the Internet—actually generate printing. The manuals, magazines, books, and other printed materials that are published in conjunction with new media are needed to explain, educate, entice, and motivate people to experiment, understand, and use these new technologies.

Our goal is this: To connect our customers to all their markets effectively, helping them get the right information to the right customers, in the right format, at the right time. To achieve this, we are implementing a new print model for our industry.

Here's what we mean. Traditional printers accept materials from the customer, print, and then distribute across the country or around the globe. At R.R. Donnelley, we are beginning to turn that model around. For customers who require simultaneous publication of timely information across the globe—especially our customers in financial markets and banking, or for software and hardware developers and publishers—we distribute information electronically, customize it, and then reproduce it in print or digital formats close to end markets.

Our customers realize tangible benefits. Products and services are delivered faster. Customers can release information simultaneously in multiple global markets. They can streamline logistics. They can reduce waste. And they can customize information to reach targeted audiences.

As we implement this new print model, we take several strengths with us: industry leadership, powerful digital technology, and our management approach, which aligns the interests of our employees with the interests of our customers and our shareholders. These are the strengths we wish to discuss in our Preface this year.

* * * *

First, our leadership position—hard won and not taken for granted.

Commercial printing is the unshakable foundation of our business. Catalogs, newspaper inserts, magazines, books, telephone directories, specialty printed products, documentation for software and other new media products, and financial printing remain strong and growing sources of our revenues and earnings and our customer relationships. These strengths help us to explore and acquire new technology, to identify and enter new businesses, to expand our business horizons, and to maintain our leadership position.

We have adopted a four-part program to accelerate our commercial print business: investment in new technology, automation and rationalization of processes, implementation of a team-based culture, and segmentation of markets.

Investment in new technology means the digitalization of the commercial print process. Installations like computer-to-plate for offset and the New Klisch Interface, a computerized cylinder-engraving system for gravure, can reduce production cycle times, speed delivery, and give our customers time to focus on their basic businesses.

Magazine publishers, for example, use digital capabilities, such as computer-to-plate, to achieve later close dates, which accommodate timely editorial content *and* allow more time to sell advertising. *Scientific American* recently published an issue on "Computers in the 21st Century" that used digital technology for every aspect of production.

When we automate or rationalize a process, we identify repetitive or manual work and streamline it. We also take outdated equipment and replace it.

As we implement a high-performance, team-based culture, a movement that extends beyond commercial printing and affects every area of our corporation, we expect to see a major payoff as our employees take more ownership of the company.

For many years, we put our commercial print customers into broad market categories. But we have discovered that the needs of a weekly magazine publisher are quite different from those of a monthly long-run consumer magazine or a short-run trade magazine publisher. By segmenting customers into smaller groups, we not only serve existing customers better, we also are discovering more about our customers and their businesses. That helps us identify and act more quickly upon potential new business opportunities; we also are better able to link customers with our expanding portfolio of services.

Industry leadership today depends on more than the ability to put ink on paper exceptionally well. We also must deliver significant improvements in value. Our announcement in 1995 of the formation of Stream International, Inc., signaled a significant step in offering more value to customers, while enhancing our leadership position. With Stream, we merged our Global Software Services business unit with Corporate Software, Inc., to create the world's largest manufacturer and reseller of computer software and services. We own approximately 80 percent of Stream International.

Stream creates a new model for this industry. It combines software manufacturing with distribution and technical support services to create a firm that offers comprehensive customer services designed to create and deliver software code and documentation.

The software services market today is highly fragmented. Software publishers often must contract with multiple firms to manufacture and distribute their products, while businesses and other software users deal with multiple companies to acquire, integrate, and manage technology. Business users are seeking less standard and more company-specific documentation.

Stream International responds to these trends by speeding time to market for the end user, by eliminating distribution redundancies and lowering costs, by enhancing security in software delivery, and by providing for the personalized creation of built-to-order, multi-vendor software solutions. Stream International is a real-world example of our industry leadership.

* * * *

Today much of print technology is based on the language of computers. Digital technology globalizes information and provides the impetus and the foundation for our international expansion.

We call this foundation our Scalable Digital Architecture. Simply put, Scalable Digital Architecture connects our customers to their markets more efficiently *and* effectively and creates new ways for them to do business.

Functionally, this means that we take a stream of data from our customers, add value to it in any number of ways, and then reproduce it in multiple print and electronic formats. Thus, we save time and money because there are fewer manual steps, and we can link information for relational marketing projects. Scalable Digital Architecture can allow us to receive product descriptions and photos, plus schematics, specifications, and pricing from a catalog retailer or direct marketer. When ready to go to market, customers can choose the information, format, and audience. Using our powerful information assembly and composition product, PowerBase™, we then create the appropriate communication vehicle: a long-run catalog; a targeted or special-interest catalog printed for an audience with specific buying patterns; a simple sell sheet; a CD-ROM version; or an on-line communication to be broadcast on the Internet.

Our Digital Division, announced in last year's Classic and with a new plant start-up in January 1995 in Memphis, concentrates on customized print-on-demand publications and works with customers to create closed-loop marketing programs that enable marketers to link a customer's buying actions with similar or related products and services. For example, through targeted direct mail, a purchaser of a DOS-based PC can quickly be offered DOS software packages and appropriate peripherals following the purchase of a PC.

Title Life Management, a digitally based program from R.R. Donnelley, enables publishers to order fewer books at an economical cost. Publishers now can efficiently print a limited quantity of books for a first edition or for reviewer copies. If the title shows promise, the publisher can then order the printing of a larger quantity.

Telephone directory, educational, and other publishers seeking new ways to disseminate information now offer information on CD-ROMs. These small discs contain huge amounts of data. With our digital capabilities, we aid publishers by creating flexible data bases, storing the information, and then outputting information for these new formats.

Advanced technology improves efficiency, but it also translates into new revenue streams for us. In the past two years, we have been awarded several large contracts based on the value represented by our sophisticated capabilities. The double-digit growth rates in Stream and in our Information Resources sector are cases in point. Also Metromail continues to be a leader in mail list development and enhancement services for the direct-mail industry. It has expanded its capabilities to offer economical lists based on ever-more-targeted data bases that pinpoint demographics, buying patterns, and even behaviors.

* * * *

R.R. Donnelley is an international company. This is not a goal. We are there today. We operate facilities in twenty countries on five continents. We offer competitive advantages to our multinational customers–high-quality, efficient print and media production, advanced technologies, and the ability to disseminate information globally.

During 1995, in addition to an expanded presence in Central Europe, Latin America, and China, we also acquired a 25 percent equity position in Tata Press, Limited, one of India's leading commercial print companies. With Tata, we expect to deliver enhanced printing technology and higher-level information and reproduction services to book and magazine publishers in India, along with international publishers serving that large market. Tata, which currently publishes yellow page directories for five major Indian cities, also positions us to participate in the country's telecommunications boom–an estimated twenty-six million new telephone lines will be installed in India by the year 2000.

* * * *

Our final strength resides within our employees. Our objective is to align the interests of employees with those of our customers and shareholders. To this end, we recently adopted an Economic Value Added business model for financial performance measurement. By focusing our attention on one factor–the value of our business–EVA™ will help ensure that we put our capital to its most productive use. EVA also links compensation directly to our performance. We also have announced targets for share ownership for more than two hundred of our top officers. We have developed consistent incentive compensation programs for all levels of the organization, and we are building our employee-owner base. Today, about two-thirds of our employees hold options on R.R. Donnelley stock.

* * * *

Our business today is increasingly one of exploration–of new technologies, into new global markets, facing exciting new challenges. We continually expand the boundaries of our business as we explore new markets around the world and as we redefine our business and create new services for existing markets. We take with us a growing cadre of successful customers, we enjoy motivated, skilled employees, and we have the resources to finance growth and exploration.

We wish you good health and good luck in the new year. May your horizons continue to beckon and to provide you with personal and professional success and happiness.

THE PUBLISHERS

December, 1995

CONTENTS

ILLUSTRATIONS

HISTORICAL ATLAS

HISTORICAL INTRODUCTION

From this window I look on Fuji San,
White with the snows of a thousand years;
To my gates ships will come from the far East
Ten thousand miles.

Attributed to Ota Dokan, warrior ruler of the Kanto region, who erected a castle at Edo (Tokyo), A.D. 1456–57.

Note: North America across the Pacific Ocean might well have been medieval Japan's "far East."

I

IN THE SUMMER of 1850, John Smith Sewall, sporting his A.B. degree from Maine's Bowdoin College, enlisted in the United States Navy, "mainly with an eye to Uncle Sam's gold to pay off college debts," as he later confided.[1] Sewall's assigned billet following basic training, not surprisingly given his education, was that of captain's clerk, a yeoman or ship's writer in modern ratings, aboard U.S.S. *Saratoga*. The *Saratoga*, captained by Commander William S. Walker, was a three-masted, square-rigged sailing ship, an old-style sloop of war with

[1]John S[mith] Sewall, *The Logbook of the Captain's Clerk: Adventures in the China Seas* (Bangor, ME: printed for the author by Chas. H. Glass & Co., 1905), p. 10. Hereafter referred to as Sewall, *Logbook*. Because of differing page sizes, the numbers cited herein refer to the pagination of this volume instead of the original publication. Sewall's book is actually a polished memoir, a work of admirable literary artistry, not a day-to-day chronicle of life aboard ship, not truly a seaman's "Logbook."

a heavy battery of twenty-two guns–eighteen 32-pounders and four 68-pounders. Her ship's company totaled 210–consisting of 22 officers and 188 crewmen. David Farragut, later celebrated as "the Union's Nelson" of Civil War renown, had commanded the *Saratoga* during the Mexican War (1846–48) before being transferred to California to establish the Mare Island Navy Yard.

Now, with Sewall aboard, *Saratoga* sailed in September from Hampton Roads, Virginia, outward bound for the South Pacific to join the East India Squadron. Four years would elapse before Sewall returned to his homeland; his doughty vessel eventually dropped anchor off Charlestown Navy Yard at Boston. Most memorably by then, Sewall had participated in Commodore Matthew Calbraith Perry's epochal expeditions of 1852–53 and 1854 to open feudal Japan to the world. And Sewall's *Saratoga,* the warship with the longest commission in Perry's squadron, proudly bore homeward the history-making Treaty of Kanagawa, which was signed on Friday, March 31, 1854, and which formally established relations between the United States of America and the Empire of Japan.[2]

Half a century later, in 1905, John S. Sewall, by then a distinguished theologian and scholar, as

[2]*Ibid.*, frontispiece and pp. 9–11, 29, 259–60; William N. Still, Jr., "David Glasgow Farragut: the Union's Nelson," James C. Bradford, ed., *Captains of the Old Steam Navy: Makers of the American Naval Tradition, 1840–1880*, (Annapolis: Naval Institute Press, 1986), pp. 166–93.

John Smith Sewall

Courtesy Bowdoin College, Brunswick, Maine

well as author of numerous articles and several books, gathered together the contemporary recollections of his navy days intending, as he stated, to "clothe them with the dignity of a book." All signers of the Treaty of Kanagawa were dead by then, also most of the ordinary actors in Commodore Perry's great drama. "As I stand by the half-century milestone and look back in quest of the two thousand officers and men who accompanied the American envoy to the Empire of the Rising Sun," Sewall mused, "it has a sobering effect to find that now less than a score of them are known to be living. I feel as if I were alone with my memories, a survivor of a vanished epoch of history." His memoir, *The Logbook of the Captain's Clerk: Adventures in the China Seas* (1905), proved, in fact, to be Sewall's final book. "If it should reach any of the survivors of the memorable expedition, let it carry a warm greeting from an old comrade," he pledged. Sewall's eyewitness account captures the original flavor of the relationship that would develop between the United States and Japan. Sewall's "logbook" likewise affords a compelling record of a young sailor's adventures in the China seas and seaports at a unique moment for all concerned, when Asia's ancient civilizations were being pried open to Western ways and technology.[3]

[3]Sewall, *Logbook*, pp. 3–5. For Sewall's other publications, see *National Union Catalog Pre-1956 Imprints*, Vol. 540, pp. 42–43; and see his biographical sketch in *Who Was Who in America*, Vol. I, 1897–1942.

Outbound from Hampton Roads and the Virginia capes, Sewall's *Saratoga* had swept southward to Rio de Janeiro, cut to the east across the Atlantic to Cape Town for supplies, sailed around the blustery Cape of Good Hope, and coursed astride the Indian Ocean through the East Indies, pausing only briefly at a Malayan island to load wood and water, until at last she reached the South China Sea to enter the western Pacific. With twenty thousand nautical miles on her log, the warship dropped anchor, in April 1851, at that "quaint old Portuguese city" of Macao on the estuary of the Pearl River a short distance below Canton. There, U.S.S. *Saratoga* would lie rolling at her anchors, often for weeks at a time in that windswept roadstead, rocking Sewall and his shipmates athwart "a choppy larruping sea." Sea duty for *Saratoga* encompassed "two years of waltzing to and fro and flitting up and down the coast, over to Manila, and up to the Madjicosima Islands," while occasionally putting ashore for respites at Macao, Hong Kong, Shanghai, or another of South China's harbors. Special assignments for the East India Squadron before the advent of Commodore Perry's expedition included pursuing mutineers and rescuing their victims, chasing innumerable pirates, even sometimes interfering in a rebellion. There proved so much to see and do that Sewall's life was never dull. "That faraway past was luminous with the hopes of youth and the promise of adventure," he recalled, "it is hallowed now with the memories of a life that is vanished and of friends that are gone."[4]

II

Vessels flying the Stars and Stripes had long been hauling cargoes, since 1784 in fact, to and from China. Grain, cheese, rum, furs, ironwares, and other manufactures, often supplemented by spices loaded in the East Indies and kegs of silver or gold coins to balance the transactions, made the lengthy journey to obtain in return precious Chinese teas, cottons, silks, lacquerwares, carpets, and porcelains. Before 1830, the smuggling of opium into China began to reap huge profits for its carriers, even when missionaries were arriving from the United States, Britain, and France with their gospel of Christian salvation.

The concurrent smuggling of opium while also proselytizing Christianity complicated the exchanges burgeoning between Chinese and Western merchants. China's efforts to stem the illicit importation of opium were crushed by the British in the Opium War of 1839–42. In addition to Canton, the only official port of entry until then, the resulting Treaty of Nanking (1842) opened the Chinese ports of Amoy, Foochow, Ningpo, and Shanghai to British trade and residence, and also ceded the city of Hong Kong to the victor.

[4]Sewall, *Logbook*, pp. 9–138.

Whalers from New Bedford, Nantucket, and their off-season Hawaiian anchorages were meanwhile roaming the bountiful fisheries newly discovered off Japan's eastern coasts and throughout the nearby waters of the Sea of Okhotsk. Japanese and Korean authorities refused, however, for two decades or so between 1835 and 1855 to permit foreigners to enter their seaports (other than the privileged Dutch or Chinese), even denying succor or rescue for tempest-tossed and shipwrecked seamen.[5] Back home, politicians proclaimed that the North Pacific Ocean should quickly become, in William H. Goetzmann's words, "a vast American lake," a bridge to the wealth of Japan and China to be underwritten by the profits of trading and whaling. The American Geographical and Statistical Society of New York City, an expansion-minded body supported in part by New England's whaling interests, pressured the U.S. government to deploy permanently a naval squadron in the western Pacific to protect Americans as well as their interests there.[6] Actually, the navy was already on station.

News of the Treaty of Nanking between China and Great Britain, hurriedly sent home by Com-

[5]Part II of this Introduction relies for its framework on Arthur Power Dudden, *The American Pacific from the Old China Trade to the Present* (New York and Oxford: Oxford University Press, 1992, 1993).

[6]William H. Goetzmann, *New Lands, New Men: America and the Second Great Age of Discovery* (New York: Viking Penguin, 1986), p. 332.

modore Lawrence Kearney, U.S.N., commanding the East India Squadron, sparked a spirited debate over the United States government's China policy—that is, rather, its lack of one. As the result, Congressman Caleb Cushing of Massachusetts arrived in the Portuguese overseas province of Macao, located sixty-five miles southeast of Canton on the estuary of the Pearl River, February 24, 1844, sent there by President John Tyler as the first United States Commissioner to China. On July 3, at Wangshia close at hand in Chinese territory, assisted by American missionaries Dr. Peter Parker, Elijah C. Bridgman, and Samuel Wells Williams, Cushing signed a treaty of amity and commerce to open diplomatic relations with China.

The Treaty of Wangshia set forth official policy:

1. Americans sought freedom to trade with the Chinese, and agreed to abide with China's regulation of that trade.
2. If other countries won specified commercial and political privileges from China, Americans expected equal treatment.
3. The United States sought no territorial gains, nor, though it was a powerful nation, did it intend to wrest any advantages from China by use of force.

Special clauses of the treaty permitted Americans to employ Chinese teachers and to purchase Chinese books recommended by Cushing's missionary advisors and interpreters.

In 1856, the second Opium War led to the British and French imposition on China of the Treaties of Tientsin (1858), to which the United States and Russia became parties through their most-favored-nation concession. China unlocked eleven more seaports; admitted foreign legations to Peking, the Ch'ing (Manchu) Dynasty's imperial capital; authorized widespread missionary activities, and legalized the importation of opium. In the renewal of hostilities in 1859, the third Opium War, British and French forces occupied Peking, burned the emperor's summer palace, and wrested still more concessions from the helpless Chinese. Americans shared almost automatically in these new advantages, including the extraterritorial privileges of immunity from local law enforcement. The United States thereby became a party to the system of "unequal treaties," which Chinese patriots of future days would so bitterly resent. Yet for decades to come, Americans assumed self-righteously that the Chinese favored them over Europeans because the United States had not won their privileges by wielding armed force.[7]

III

From the end of the War of 1812 to the Civil War, the spectacular growth of the nation's oceangoing commerce greatly expanded the size and scope of

[7]Dudden, *The American Pacific*, pp. 7–8.

the U.S. Navy's duties. Worldwide, for its prestigious Mediterranean Squadron, as well as the other forces patrolling African, American, and Asian waters, the navy required between forty and fifty steam and sail vessels. Naval commanders not only had to safeguard American lives, property, and overseas trade routes, and to identify potential sources of profit by obtaining commercial and nautical information, they were expected to negotiate diplomatic bargains and open new markets. Naval technology was simultaneously undergoing an historic transformation. For three centuries, ships and armaments had changed but little. Now propulsion changed from sail to steam, hulls from wood to iron or steel, ordnance from muzzle-loading smoothbore cannons to breech-loading rifled guns, and projectiles from solid shot to detonating shells. Although the American Navy of that day never produced a national hero to rival Horatio Nelson, the men leading the way into the Age of Steam featured such giants as the American naval officers David Farragut and Matthew C. Perry.[8]

Operating in China's waters under the Treaty of Wangshia, the East India Squadron, which included John Sewall's *Saratoga*, was but a singular part of the navy's global picture, and pursuing

[8]Bradford, ed., *Captains of the Old Steam Navy*, pp. xi–xv. For background, consult James C. Bradford, ed., *Command under Sail…, 1775–1850,* (Annapolis, Naval Institute Press, 1985).

pirates only one of its routine duties. Piracy, once well-nigh universal, concentrated itself those days off East Asia's mainland in coastal waters bordering the South China Sea throughout China's harbors, inlets, and rivers. Pirates also bedeviled shipping in the waters of the southern Philippines off Mindanao and the Sulu Archipelago, as well as inside the Straits of Malacca between the Malay Peninsula and the Dutch East Indies. Chinese pirates swarmed along the merchantmen's route between Singapore and Hong Kong. Many fishermen took up piracy whenever their catches dwindled. Ships linking Macao with the new British colony of Hong Kong and Canton farther up the Pearl River, which the Chinese still called Zhu Jiang, were particularly vulnerable. Zhu Jiang was plagued by pirates. Pirate chieftains could swiftly muster fifty or more armed junks for their savage raids. Such fleets formed and evaporated like fogbanks. As the pirate admiral Changpaou colorfully remarked, "We are like vapors blown by the wind; we are like waves of the sea roused by whirlwind; like broken bamboo sticks on the sea, we float and sink–without rest." Suppressing pirates to protect commerce in Chinese waters became a regular assignment for the United States Navy, as well as for the other treaty powers.[9]

Japan was another story altogether, for attempts

[9]Pegram Harrison, "*Fighting Pirates on the Zhu Jiang*," *Naval History*, Vol. IX (March/April 1995), pp. 35–40.

to deal with that country's authorities had invariably been contemptuously spurned. In July 1846, Commodore James Biddle, U.S.N., aboard the ninety-gun *Columbia* accompanied by the sloop-of-war *Vincennes*, anchored in the Bay of Edo (Tokyo) to negotiate with Japan a treaty of friendship and commerce. Biddle carelessly allowed hordes of armed guard boats to surround his warships and Japanese sailors to board and inspect them. Lacking an interpreter, Biddle dealt personally with several minor Japanese officials, and even entrusted President James K. Polk's official letter to one such functionary. The emperor's representatives ashore thereupon rejected Polk's letter and summarily ordered Biddle to sail at once. Crestfallen, Commodore Biddle made ready to depart, only to suffer further humiliation when his tormentors towed his warships out to sea.

However, in 1849, Commander Thomas Glynn boldly sailed U.S.S. *Preble* into Nagasaki harbor, to demand the release of fifteen stranded American whalers being detained there. Glynn threatened to bombard the city if the seamen were not promptly set free, which, following two days of wrangling, they were. On returning home, Glynn urged that another expedition be sent to open Japan. Businessmen and senior naval officers, searching for new ways to protect the country's whaling fleet and expand trade overall as well, backed up Glynn's appeal. In agreement, President Millard Fillmore's administration chose Matthew C. Perry to take command of the East India Squadron for this important enterprise.

Matthew Calbraith Perry (1794–1858) came from a distinguished naval family. His father, an officer, served both in the War of Independence and in the undeclared naval war against France (1798–1800). Matthew C. Perry and, likewise, his four brothers joined the navy, among them Oliver Hazard Perry, destined to become the heroic victor of the Battle of Lake Erie in the War of 1812. Early in his career, Matthew Perry played an important role in the transformation of naval technology. Eager to prove steam warships practicable, he founded the navy's engineering corps, becoming credited later, perhaps with some exaggeration, as the "father of the steam navy." Nevertheless, he rose to the rank of captain aboard wooden sailing ships. In 1843, he took command of the Africa Squadron to police the slave trade and protect Liberia's settlements of freed slaves founded by the American Colonization Society. At the outbreak of the Mexican War, he captained the side-wheeler *Mississippi*, a steam-powered warship he designed, until he assumed full command, in 1847, over the Gulf Squadron. In the capture of Vera Cruz, Perry ably led his well-trained gun crews ashore to assist General Winfield Scott. Perry and his men went on to seize the upriver towns of Tuxpan and Tabasco (present-day Villahermosa). Dubbed "Old Bruin" for his bear-like, gruffly barked orders, Perry won wide respect for his diligent, efficient, and courageous leadership afloat or ashore. Wisely, the navy, in 1851, selected Perry to take charge of the delicate mission planned to open diplomatic relations with the Empire of Japan. Japan, within her insular empire under the feudal Tokugawa Shogunate, had largely secluded herself from the outside world since 1639, with only Dutch and Chinese traders admitted into a single, restricted port of entry at Nagasaki and Christian missionaries wholly barred.[10]

With energy and painstaking care, Perry turned to his greatest undertaking. He requested a substantially enlarged squadron, three ships being added at once with others to follow, until, in due course, Perry would command a flotilla of ten vessels, a concentration of American strength unprecedented in Asian waters. Perry also picked able lieutenants whom he knew firsthand, including Commanders Franklin Buchanan, Sidney S. Lee, and Joel Abbot, skippers respectively of the new steamers *Susquehanna* and *Mississippi* and the old, wind-driven *Macedonian*. Perry also learned as much about Asia and Japan as he could. He read

[10]John H. Schroeder, "Matthew Calbraith Perry: Antebellum Precursor of the Old Steam Navy," in Bradford, ed., *Captains of the Old Steam Navy*, pp. 3–13*ff*. For the capture of Vera Cruz during the Mexican War, see The Lakeside Classics edition written by George Ballentine, *Autobiography of an English Soldier in the United States Army*, edited by William H. Goetzmann (Chicago: R.R. Donnelley & Sons Company, 1986).

extensively on these exotic subjects while consulting with the scholarly Philipp Franz von Siebold, an experienced expert. From fellow naval officers who had voyaged into the western Pacific and from New Bedford's whaling captains, he gathered additional vital information. By the time he was ready to proceed, he had made himself exceptionally knowledgeable about the history, culture, and folkways of the Japanese people and the institutions of Japanese society. Finally, Perry stockpiled gifts to impress upon the Japanese the many achievements of his nation.

Perry now convinced his superiors to make the diplomatic mission to Japan his primary responsibility, not merely supplementary to his routine duties as the commanding officer of the East India Squadron. He gained permission from Secretary of the Navy John P. Kennedy and Secretary of State Daniel Webster to draft his own diplomatic instructions. When approved, these instructions defined three major objectives for Perry's mission. The expedition's purposes would be to gain a treaty to: 1) provide protection for American ships and their crews wrecked or endangered by stormy weather in Japanese waters; 2) permit American ships to obtain water, provisions, and fuel, and, if necessary, repair and refit in Japanese harbors; and 3) allow the survey and exploration of the coastal waters surrounding Japan. To achieve his objectives, Perry's superiors authorized him to employ his "whole force," though he was cautioned, almost in the same breath, that his enterprise must be of a "pacific character." Perry's orders read to conduct himself as "courteous and conciliatory, but at the same time firm and decided." He might resort to force only in self-defense or "to resent an act of personal violence" against himself or any of his men. He carried a letter to the Emperor of Japan from President Millard Fillmore.[11]

IV

Ready at last for the momentous enterprise, Commodore Matthew Calbraith Perry got underway in November 1852 aboard his flagship, the steam frigate U.S.S. *Mississippi*. The side-wheeler tracked down the Atlantic Ocean around Africa's southern tip via the Cape of Good Hope following the time-honored route of the East Indiamen, sailed through the Indian Ocean into the western Pacific, and dropped her anchors at Hong Kong in April 1853. Three of the commodore's warships were awaiting him there. U.S.S. *Saratoga* was one of these ships, with John S. Sewall, the author of our *Logbook*, aboard. Perry intended to prepare a comprehensive report of his expedition. Especially, he hoped to convey the true appearance of Japanese society, commerce, fisheries, and agriculture. Two artists also were accompanying him. Most of the

[11]Schroeder, "Perry," pp. 14–16.

report's extraordinary illustrations would be the work of Wilhelm Heine, a twenty-five-year-old native of Germany, an immigrant who had resided for only three years in the United States before shipping out with Perry. Many others would be the work of Eliphalet Brown, Jr., a daguerreotype photographer from Manhattan, while illustrations initialed W. T. Peters or H. Patterson more than likely were later redrawn by these little-known New York artists from Brown's daguerreotypes.[12]

Commodore Perry's arrival on the seventh of April, Sewall tells us, produced the usual flurry of "rumors" and "scuttlebutt" that spontaneously throughout the navy, like a seagull winging ahead of a ship's bowspray, precedes any dependable information whatever. "When the air cleared, the one fact left which specially concerned us," Sewall went on, "was that the *Saratoga* would be detained to form a part of the great expedition. The appointed term of our cruise was up, indeed, or would be by the time we could reach home. But the squadron was small at best, and the commodore could ill afford to spare a single ship; and on our own part a

[12]Francis L. Hawks, comp., *Narrative of the Expedition of an American Squadron to the China Seas and Japan Performed in the Years 1852, 1853, and 1854 under the Command of Commodore M. C. Perry, United States Navy*, 3 Vols. (Washington: A.O.P. Nicholson by order of Congress, 1856); originally published in *Senate Executive Documents* No. 34 of 33d Congress, 2d Session. Hereafter referred to as Hawks, *Narrative of the Expedition*.

visit to that mysterious land was too big a thing to miss." So it was settled. Sewall's warship was ordered to Japan along with Perry. Sewall's place on the *Saratoga*'s muster-roll would simply be that of his captain's clerk. Nonetheless, "in close relations, with a good-natured commander, the clerk may have great advantages of observation," Sewall confided about the *Saratoga*'s skipper, Commander William S. Walker. The adventures chronicled in his *Logbook*, he averred, are "the testimony of an eyewitness to the principal scenes described."

Years later, Sewall was to learn more about the documents Commodore Perry had brought with him. No less a figure than Hannibal Hamlin, his "neighbor and friend," became his informant. Hamlin served as Maine's longtime United States Senator and Abraham Lincoln's first-term Vice-President during the Civil War years. During his first term in Congress, Hamlin interested himself in expanding trade with Asian countries. He urged Secretary of State Webster, in 1850, "to open up amicable relations and negotiate commercial treaties with these nations." In November 1852, Edward Everett, Webster's successor, reworked the instrument Webster had drafted but never sent, whereupon President Fillmore added his signature. To impress the Japanese most favorably, as the Americans hoped, three copies of Fillmore's letter to the Mikado were handsomely engrossed in English, Dutch, and Chinese–that is, handwritten large as befitted so important an official document. Enclosed in "a sumptuous gold case," the gold case was itself shrouded in a coffer of rosewood. This was the "precious missive" Perry was carrying when he took charge of the East India Squadron.[13]

Beforehand in Washington, Perry had advised his superiors of the importance of acquiring "ports of refuge and supply" as bases for entry into Japan. At Shanghai, Perry transferred his commodore's flag to the steamship *Susquehanna*, and, in mid-May 1853, he ordered his flotilla to proceed south of Japan for a dress rehearsal, to Great Lew Chew Island (Liu Ch'iu, the Chinese name for Okinawa, meaning the great island, within the Japanese-controlled archipelago, later to be renamed the Ryukyu Islands). Sewall's *Saratoga*, which carried Dr. S. Wells Williams, the expedition's interpreter, caught up with the *Susquehanna* and the *Mississippi* entering the port of Naha. The *Plymouth* appeared a few days afterward. With the storeships *Supply* and *Caprice* included, Perry's tiny armada was fully assembled. His rehearsal could take place as intended.

To commence, Commodore Perry disdained even to acknowledge the presence of any of the local authorities, who were attempting to welcome his ships, until the ruler's Japanese regent himself

[13]Sewall, *Logbook*, pp. 10–11, 141–42; Charles Eugene Hamlin, *Life and Times of Hannibal Hamlin*, (Cambridge: The Riverside Press, 1899, repr. 1971).

called on him. Then, overriding that dignitary's horrified protests, Perry haughtily proclaimed his intention to visit the royal palace at Shuri. To dramatize his exalted purpose, he was conveyed to the palace in an elaborate sedan chair built hurriedly by a ship's carpenter, accompanied by the flotilla's smartly uniformed bandsmen. He visited the palace at length, feasting at the regent's invitation, until he and his entourage returned to their ships. Over the next two weeks, his officers and crews made themselves fully at home. They explored the island, surveyed its coastal waters, and established a shelter for Americans on shore.

Next, *Susquehanna* and *Saratoga* sailed off in a northeasterly direction bound for the Bonin Islands. Perry had readily grasped the islands' strategic significance lying, as they did, astride the great circle route from Honolulu to the ports of South China.

Sometime earlier, thirty or more colonists from Hawaii headed by Nathaniel Savoy, a far-ranging New Englander, had settled themselves in the islands at Port Lloyd. Perry raised the American flag, laid down a code of laws, and arranged Savoy's election as chief magistrate. He also purchased a waterfront property for future service as a coal depot. In time, he would enter an official United States claim to sovereignty over these islands. Perry wanted Lew Chew and the Bonins for larger purposes than convenient bases to open up Japan. He believed he was establishing two permanent American "ports of refuge and supply" for whalers, merchantmen, and naval vessels. Returned once more to Naha, Perry drilled his forces for the great task to come. He sent shore parties to forage throughout Lew Chew and to gather all the information about Japan they could uncover.

On July 2, 1853, "Old Bruin" Perry ordered his four warships out of Naha harbor for the six-day journey to Japan. He determined for the success of his delicate undertaking to present "a resolute attitude" toward Japan's officials. He resolved to steer clear of the mistakes of prior adventurers, instead "to demand as a right, and not to solicit as a favor, those acts of courtesy which are due from one civilized nation to another." Perry likewise made up his mind "to allow none of those petty annoyances which had been unsparingly visited upon those who had preceded him, and to disregard the acts as well as the threats of the authorities, if they in the least conflicted with his own sense of what was due to the dignity of the American flag." For all hands, their great moment was fast approaching. Sewall recorded the departures of the two steam frigates towing the sailing ships from the harbor, as usual: "The *Saratoga* took her place in tow of the *Susquehanna* as before, and the *Plymouth* in tow of the *Mississippi*. The *Supply* storeship was left for the time at anchor in Napa[Naha] harbor, and the *Caprice* under command of Lieutenant William L.

Maury was sent to Shanghai." Perry's expedition mustered a total of sixty-one guns and 977 officers and men.[14]

Japan, as Perry's small fleet drew near, had for some seven centuries been ruled by warrior lords (*daimyo*) and their aristocratic vassals (*samurai*), under feudal arrangements similar in numerous aspects to the ties between lords and vassals that had governed Europe for ages before the sixteenth century. Feudalism in western Europe largely disappeared following the Renaissance, when it gave way before the all-encompassing powers wielded by such rulers as the Hapsburg Emperor Charles V and France's Bourbon King Louis XIV. Feudalism in Japan, however, endured vigorously for another three hundred years. By then, the West had undergone England's Glorious Revolution of 1689, the American Revolution of 1776, and the French Revolution of 1789, while the Industrial Revolution continued apace to reshape the fundamental circumstances of human existence. From around 1614 until just after the American Civil War, a *shogun*, or military overlord, ruled Japan from Edo, the eastern capital. The emperor at Kyoto, though still recognized as the source of imperial legitimacy, was almost powerless, serving merely during this period as a figurehead. Japan's emperors were traditionally bypassed on worldly matters.

[14]Sewall, *Logbook*, pp. 147–67, 169; Hawks, *Narrative of the Expedition*, Vol. I, p. 235; Schroeder, "Perry," pp. 16–17.

The office of *shogun* became hereditary under the leaders of the powerful Tokugawa clan, who proceeded to withdraw Japan from almost all external contacts into a self-protective, hermit-like seclusion. Thus, by their extraordinary action, the Tokugawas achieved nearly two-and-a-half centuries of peace and stability. This Tokugawa Shogunate comprised, in a cultural sense, a golden age of remarkable accomplishment, especially in intellectual development, the fine arts and crafts, a flourishing commerce, and a very satisfying domestic prosperity. But it was a shadowy time of ruthless repression, when Edo's overlords exercised arbitrary control through their extensive and efficient deployments of the secret police system.

By 1850, Japanese society embodied a comparatively tranquil and well-educated population of thirty million individuals, with a level of literacy more than likely superior to the United States and most of Europe. More than one million people dwelled in Edo alone. If anything, Japan's inferiority to the West was singularly technological rather than cultural. Japan's rulers wanted only that their country be left alone.

Unfortunately, the tidings from China grew evermore disturbing. British warships during the first Opium War (1839–42) had forced Chinese authorities to open several previously forbidden seaports to foreign traders. Russians, French, Americans, Germans, and other "foreign devils" immediately poured into China, invoking their countries' most-favored-nation treaties with Great Britain to partake of these same advantages for themselves. And to make the situation even worse, the Taiping Rebellion (1850–64), a massive revolt against the ruling Ch'ing Dynasty, was spreading violently throughout the eastern valley of the Yangtze River. The once-proud Chinese found themselves being pressed to open more ports, to grant humiliating rights of extraterritoriality to the despised foreigners, and even to welcome Christian missionaries. The Japanese feared they might fall prey to similar impositions.

Well might they worry, for cloistered Japan's real defenses were threadbare and antiquated. The Tokugawa clan fecklessly for years installed a string of indolent rulers who had delegated their irksome day-to-day responsibilities to fawning courtiers. Aroused *daimyo* and their loyal *samurai* followers, alarmed by the signs of decay, were questioning the very legitimacy of the shogunate. The nationalist impulse to restore full sovereign authority to the emperor at Kyoto quickly gained momentum. In truth, Japan's evident unreadiness to thwart the aggressive Westerners, who were equipped with the most advanced armaments the world had ever seen, was dooming the shogunate even before Perry's squadron hove into sight. Perry's steam-powered warships, *Susquehanna* and *Mississippi*, spewing black clouds of coal smoke nevertheless afforded the Americans a tremendous psychological advantage for, until this very moment, scarcely any Japanese had ever seen such terrifying apparitions. Indeed, the months ahead were going to be both extremely important and very exciting for the Japanese and their unwelcome callers.[15]

V

On Friday morning, the eighth of July 1853, Perry's lookouts sighted Japan's shores flanking the broad entrance to the Bay of Edo. A rousing cry of "Land ho!" echoed from ship to ship. "We rushed on deck," Sewall remembered. "There it was, at last. There it was, a dark silent cloud on the northern horizon, a *terra incognita*, still shrouded in mystery, still inspiring the imagination with an indefinable awe, just as it had years ago in the studies of our childhood at school." There, as the mists of the morning dissolved into the air, lay the Empire of Japan, "a living picture of hills and valleys, fields and hedges, groves, orchards, and forests." Beyond the checkpoint at Uraga, Japan's villages appeared at a distance, bulwarked as they were by fortifications, to be less densely congested than China's

[15]Valuable still is E. H. Norman, *Japan's Emergence as a Modern State* (New York: Institute of Pacific Relations, 1940), reprinted in *Origins of the Modern Japanese State: Selected Writings of E. H. Norman*, ed., John W. Dower (New York: Pantheon, 1975), Chap. II, "The Background of the Meiji Restoration." See Dudden, *The American Pacific*, pp. 5–11, 17–18, 113–16, 136–39.

and with streets a bit wider. Boats skimmed about the squadron's anchorage, some rowed or paddled by strange-looking boatmen, others wafted along on the light breeze. Towering most majestically, some forty miles away, "like a giant man-at-arms standing sentry over the scene," soared the snow-covered, volcanic cone of the "matchless mountain," sacred Fujiyama.

Suddenly, swarms of junks and guard vessels surrounded the American ships. But this time, the Japanese sailors found themselves being fended off by Perry's seamen, not allowed, as unwisely they had been by Commodore Biddle, to secure lines to the American warships nor board them. Commodore Perry did not come this far to be intimidated. He maintained to the Japanese that he was not a pirate and need not be guarded against. "They pleaded Japanese law. He replied with American law. They still insisted," Sewall wrote of this tense moment. "Whereupon he clinched the American side of the argument with the notice that if the boats were not off in fifteen minutes he should be obliged to open his batteries and sink them." His threat, "was entirely convincing," Sewall observed dryly, "and the guard boats stood not on the order of their going but betook themselves to the shelter of the shore."

So it was that the expedition's first day at anchor in the Bay of Edo closed on the peaceful beauty of a starlit night. There was a singular exception, as

Sewall recalled—"a brilliant display of meteoric light in the sky during the midwatch, an omen which terribly alarmed our friends on shore, as portending that the very heavens themselves were enlisted on the side of the barbarians." Commodore Perry reflected on this comet (for a comet it probably was) in his journal: "The ancients would have construed this remarkable appearance of the heavens as a favorable omen for any enterprise they had undertaken. It may be so construed by us, as we pray God that our present attempt to bring a singular and isolated people into the family of civilized nations may succeed without resort to bloodshed."[16]

Next day, while Commodore Perry secluded himself aloofly in his quarters, his subordinates assisted the regional vice governor, Nagashima Saberoske, to board the *Susquehanna*. They informed Nagashima that Perry was bearing a letter from the President of the United States of America to the Emperor of Japan, which he would hand over to the highest authorities only at Uraga, not at Nagasaki as the regent was insisting, and further, if the Japanese balked, the Americans would proceed immediately to Edo to the imperial palace itself. To emphasize his determination after Nagashima's leave-taking, the commodore ordered navigational surveys made of the waters at hand, which persuaded the Japanese, after considerable haggling, to

[16]Sewall, *Logbook*, pp. 168–75, 179; Hawks, *Narrative of the Expedition*, Vol. I, p. 236.

Conference Room in Hakodate; from The Expedition of an American Squadron

Courtesy The Beverly R. Robinson Collection, United States Naval Academy Museum, Annapolis, Maryland

agree to accept Millard Fillmore's letter on shore at nearby Kurihama. Months had elapsed since Perry sailed from Norfolk to attempt to open Japan. On March 4, 1853, Franklin Pierce was inaugurated as the new President of the United States to succeed Fillmore. This would make little difference, if any, for shaping these events about to take place on the far side of the earth.

Sewall's observations are fascinating. Discussions between the Americans and the Japanese generally occurred in the Dutch language through Anton L. C. Portman, an able interpreter hired by the Americans in Shanghai. Initially, the Americans innocently assumed that the isolated Japanese must know little about the world outside. Yet one Japanese promptly revealed himself as well informed about the geography of the United States, another correctly identified the model of the big gun mounted on the *Susquehanna*'s quarterdeck, and still another adjudged that sextants of the finest quality were manufactured only in London not Paris. (Later, in China, Sewall would learn for himself that Japanese printers regularly republished textbooks that missionaries were distributing. Much of the surprising knowledge about America, for example, was copied directly from the work of a missionary, Elijah C. Bridgman, and his *History of the United States*.)

On July 14, at daybreak, *Susquehanna* and *Mississippi* steamed into the little bay at Kurihama and positioned themselves to bombard the coastal fortifications if necessary, while thousands of warriors and spectators clamored menacingly along the shore. To the thunder of a thirteen-gun salute and preceded by more than 250 officers and enlisted men, "well befeathered in full uniform and armed to the teeth," with a ship's band shrilling "Hail Columbia!," Perry landed from his barge personally to deliver the president's letter. "Two boys dressed for the ceremony preceded the Commodore, bearing, in an envelope of scarlet cloth, the boxes which contained his credentials and the president's letter," the official report relates. "These documents, of folio size, were beautifully written on vellum, and not folded, but bound in blue silk velvet. Each seal, attached by cords of interwoven gold and silk with pendant tassels, was encased in a circular box six inches in diameter and three in depth wrought of pure gold. Each of the documents, together with its seal, was placed in a box of rosewood about a foot long, with lock, hinges, and mountings all of gold. On either side of the Commodore marched a tall, well-formed Negro, who, armed to the teeth, acted as his personal guard." Chosen for the occasion, these black seamen were the two very best-looking fellows that the squadron could muster for the desired effect.

Two ornately attired imperial princes awaited the commodore. These were Toda, Prince of Izu, fiftyish in his apparent age, and Ito, Prince of Iwami, looking ten to fifteen years older. They wore robes of weighty silk brocade ornamented with elegantly wrought gold and silver figurines. Between the two sides, the official interpreters located themselves, one a Japanese scholar on his knees bowing low, the other, S. Wells Williams, LL.D., who was "erect and dignified," himself a distinguished sinologist, as well as author, and longtime missionary in China.

Together with President Fillmore's demand for a treaty to open Japan to commerce and international tenets of behavior, including diplomatic relations and rescuing shipwrecked seamen, Fillmore had ostentatiously bragged in his letter to the emperor that, "Our ships can go from California to Japan in eighteen days." In reply, the Japanese presented a scroll to the Americans acknowledging receipt of the president's letter, yet denouncing its "impertinence," and, while notifying Perry he must depart, declared no further negotiations could occur.

Deflated somewhat, the commodore agreed to leave within two or three days, but flatly rejected a tender of equal trading rights with the beleaguered Dutch at Nagasaki. He courteously offered, nevertheless, to convey any messages the Japanese government might choose to send with him to Lew Chew or Canton. Perry added that he would return the following spring, quite possibly with additional warships, and, at this pronouncement, the extraordinary encounter ended. Perry and his men returned to their ships without interference.

Transferring his flag to the *Mississippi*, Perry steamed boldly up the bay as far as the outskirts of the city of Edo before turning back, to demonstrate his refusal to be intimidated. A simple farewell ceremony took place near Uraga on July 16, with modest gifts being exchanged, before the Americans departed next day for Naha. Perry decided, in choosing to leave Japan rather than await a reply to President Fillmore's letter, that he required time to reprovision his vessels, to add more warships to his squadron, and to tend to any problems that might have arisen in China or elsewhere. Time, he realized also, would give the Japanese ample opportunity to conduct thoroughgoing deliberations among themselves. Perry had avoided Commodore Biddle's errors. His meticulous preparations, together with his thoughtfulness, formality, and firmness unquestionably delivered the message to the Japanese that he could not be brushed off by their traditional tactics of delay. "This was not child's play. It was not an assumption of pomp inconsistent with republican simplicity," wrote Sewall, who thoroughly understood the drama he was witnessing. "Commodore Perry was dealing with an oriental potentate according to oriental ideas. He showed his sagacity in doing so. At the time, he was fifty-nine years old, a man of splendid physique and commanding presence." It is obvious that Captain's Clerk John Smith Sewall greatly admired his squadron's commodore. Thus, this very first phase of Perry's expedition to open Japan had been accomplished. As if to an oyster, the plucky commodore had deftly insinuated his blade. Japan was going to open up peaceably. It was being well done.[17]

VI

From Japan, U.S.S. *Saratoga* sailed to China, where, in August, she moored off Shanghai's foreign settlements. The embankment, Sewall noted, afforded "a scene of busy prosperity," with residences facing the water, clean wide streets, warehouses bulging with the products of trade and, flying protectively over all, the flags of the consulates, British, American, Spanish, and French. After spending weeks under tight discipline, the warship's officers and crewmen on liberty at last could go ashore to relax and enjoy themselves.

But suddenly, after a restful month, the terrible fury of the Taiping Rebellion burst upon them "like the proverbial thunderbolt," in Sewall's depiction, "out of a clear sky." "Taiping," he later reflected ruefully, "means Great Peace, a term not altogether appropriate for the wholesale plundering, ravaging, and slaughtering that came to be perpetrated under its banners." The massive uprising of the Taiping hordes, which nearly overturned the Ch'ing Dynasty before disintegrating, erupted originally out

[17] Sewall, *Logbook*, pp. 179–200; Hawks, *Narrative of the Expedition*, Vol. I, pp. 254–55, 272–73; Dudden, *The American Pacific*, p. 18; Schroeder, "Perry," pp. 17–19.

of Christian fanaticism, yet it also embodied a classic expression of peasant revolt. Taiping's prophet was Hung Hsui-ch'uan, who was preaching a gospel of Old Testament Protestant Christianity incendiarily blended with fraternal appeals for Chinese patriotism and democratic egalitarianism. Hung's charismatic message won him multitudes of adherents, especially among the millions of impoverished peasants. The Taiping movement raced like wildfire through the eastern valley of the Yangtze River to capture Nanking and threaten Shanghai. "For five months," Sewall recorded, "we were curious spectators of a Chinese war, and the scenes we witnessed left ineffaceable memories. We began with sympathy for a new cause. We ended with sympathy for the lacerated empire." Long before the end of the Taiping Rebellion, however, Commodore Perry summoned Sewall's *Saratoga* away from Shanghai. The momentous second act of the Japan expedition was ready to open.

Months later, long after the *Saratoga* sailed away, Shanghai's rich merchants and businessmen raised a foreign legion for self-protection led by Frederick T. Ward, an adventuresome Yankee from Salem, Massachusetts. The legion's spectacular triumphs over the Taiping forces would earn from China's grateful emperor by 1862 the title of "Ever-Victorious Army." When Ward died of his battle wounds, his command passed to another American, Henry A. Burgevine, a shady conspirator who promptly purloined forty thousand silver dollars for himself. Consequently, Burgevine was relieved of his duty by the soon-to-become-famous British officer Charles George "Chinese" Gordon. The spreading destruction of life and property helped, in 1859, to bring on the third Opium War. The Summer Palace in Peking was torched by the British and French, who then seized advantage of the chaos to wrest additional privileges for themselves. The revisions of Great Britain's and France's treaties with China, in 1860, opened up eleven more ports to them, and granted even broader freedoms for their missionaries, whereupon British and French forces joined the emperor's armies to subdue the Taiping rebels. The Americans promptly followed the Anglo-French lead in winning their own treaty revisions, once more riding piggyback on the great powers.[18]

VII

Early in February of 1854, Commodore Perry's squadron headed again toward Japan, returning several weeks earlier than Perry intended when he sailed away the previous summer. The commodore was beginning to fear from rumors—needlessly, it proved—that his British, French, or Russian rivals might beat him to the opening up of Japan. The

[18]Immanuel C.Y. Hsü, *The Rise of Modern China*, 5th ed., (New York: Oxford University Press, 1995), pp. 214–15, 221–56.

Navy Department meanwhile had beefed up his strength. The East India Squadron's black-hulled combat vessels included a third steam-powered frigate, U.S.S. *Powhatan*, just arrived to join *Mississippi* and *Susquehanna*. Besides the older warships, the *Saratoga*, *Plymouth*, *Vandalia*, and *Macedonian*, plus the storeships *Southampton*, *Supply*, and *Lexington*, Perry's flotilla, whenever all of his ships assembled together, now numbered ten. In reserve, two hired vessels, the steamer *Queen* and the supply barque *Caprice*, provided additional strength and flexibility. After the Kurihama conference in the previous July, Perry's original four ships, mission accomplished, had split up outside Tokyo Bay, the *Saratoga* ordered to Shanghai and the rest back to Lew Chew.

Perry himself had returned at first to Naha on the island of Great Lew Chew, where he renewed his tactic of applying indirect pressure against the Japanese through the barrage of demands he made on their hapless local regent. Once more, he requested that a coal storage shed be erected there, and insisted on permission for his officers and sailors to roam freely about the island. For emphasis, a ship's carpenter received instructions to inspect and repair the sedan chair Perry used during his initial stopover, as if the commodore had determined to make another presumptuous appearance at the royal palace. Perry also announced his intention for an American occupation of Lew Chew, should his

U.S.S. Plymouth

U.S.S. Powhatan

Illustrations Courtesy National Archives, College Park, Maryland

mission to open Japan fail. Hastily this time, the Japanese-controlled regent complied with his requests, whereupon Perry promptly departed for China to make additional preparations for returning to Japan. In China, indications worried him of Russian, French, and British expeditions preparing to enter Japan, which speeded up his own readiness for a midwinter departure. By the end of January, most of Perry's squadron had regrouped in Naha harbor.[19]

On February 11, Commodore Perry's ships reentered the Bay of Edo. News of the emperor's recent death had already reached Perry from the governor general of the Netherlands East Indies in Batavia, who, serving as an intermediary, conveyed Japan's request to Perry that he postpone his intended return due to the necessity for staging appropriate mourning ceremonials and the time required to arrange the successor's installation as emperor. Perry objected. In refusing to postpone his mission, Perry artfully expressed the hope that Japan's rulers "will not be disposed to throw any serious obstacle in the way of a friendly understanding between the two nations," for, as he argued, they have become well satisfied by the propositions of President Fillmore, which he himself had the honor of presenting to them. On February 13, the squadron stood up the bay once more to anchor again off Uraga.

[19]Sewall, *Logbook*, p. 199; Hawks, *Narrative of the Expedition*, Vol. I, pp. 272–73, 320; Schroeder, "Perry," pp. 18–19.

The local dignitaries welcomed them hospitably this time, with the gladsome tidings that five commissioners headed by Prince Councillor Hayashi had been appointed and were ready to negotiate with Perry. Just the same, the inevitable arguments arose over in which location the talks might take place, until, abruptly, the Japanese gave up their insistence on Uraga to propose Yokohama as the site instead, up the bay barely fifteen miles short of the capital, and Perry agreed. On March 4, U.S.S. *Saratoga*, laden with gifts for the Japanese, arrived to rejoin the squadron. Both parties were now ready for serious business. The climate between them this time was friendly, free of hostility, and wholly auspicious.[20]

Commodore Perry's second landing, on March 8, 1854, was even more spectacular than his first: a seventeen-gun salute acclaiming his ambassadorial status, a parade of five hundred festooned officers, sailors, and marines all fully armed, three armed bands proudly playing "The Star-Spangled Banner," and a courteous reception by the awaiting Japanese. Delivering the imperial reply to Perry's demands of the previous July, Japan's commissioners consented to assist shipwrecked American seamen and vessels in distress, also to supply water, provisions, and coal at one harbor to be designated. Coal might be

[20]Sewall, *Logbook*, pp. 239–62; Hawks, *Narrative of the Expedition*, Vol. I, pp. 309–10, 321–42; Schroeder, "Perry," pp. 18–19.

obtained meanwhile at Nagasaki. The Japanese, in addition, expressed a willingness to sell or barter anything available within Japan's island empire that ships might want. Negotiations and festivities now proceeded virtually nonstop, with Perry and his lieutenants bargaining item by item over the extent of the commercial concessions under consideration, plus the numbers and locations of ports to be opened. Throughout, the Japanese deferred to Perry as "Admiral," not comprehending his lower rank of Commodore, a position unknown to them. "And though the American demands were contested inch by inch," Sewall recorded, "yet it was done with good nature and the commissioners almost invariably yielded."

On March 13, Commodore Perry presented his nation's gifts to his Japanese hosts, a staggering array of American manufactures and products, featuring working demonstrations of the miniature steam railway, the electric telegraph, a telescope, a camera, clocks, a small brass Dahlgren howitzer especially useful for firing salutes, as well as multiple examples of small arms and farm machinery. America's generosity was followed, March 24, by the Mikado's officials reciprocating in kind with precious works of fine artistry and elegant craftsmanship. A festive air prevailed. Sumo wrestlers, musicians, and minstrels entertained hundreds of American officers and crewmen and crowds of onlooking Japanese. Welcome now, visitors flocked to board the American ships. "They liked our dinners," Sewall noted, "they took very kindly, sometimes convivially, to our brandies and wines." On shore, the commodore and the commissioners staged lavish banquets for each other. It was John Sewall's good fortune to be included at one of the Japanese feasts. "The dinner was abundant," he recalled. "To our Saxon [*sic*] appetites, it was toothsome, and what with chopsticks and our own fingers and penknives we wrestled with it in masterly fashion." The menu offered soups, vegetables, oysters, crabs, boiled eggs, pickled fish, seaweed jelly, as well as several dishes not identifiable to the Americans. Drinks served were tea and *sake*, Japan's strong, colorless rice wine. Dinner over, the hosts led the sailors back to their landing boats, presenting them, as they left for the anchored ships, with large sacks of rice–enough for the entire fleet.

During the closing negotiations over the next few days, various matters, already agreed to in principle, were definitively settled. The seaports of Shimoda and Hakodate having been accepted as suitable for American use, Shimoda was chosen for the United States consul's residence, and the problem of the distances around these two ports, where Americans might extend their travels into the countryside, was settled besides. Also made "perfectly plain," at least for the time being, was the absolute prohibition throughout Japan against any permanent residence for Americans with their families.

Hakodate from the Bay; from The Expedition of an American Squadron

Courtesy University of Chicago Library

American and Japanese interpreters, in close cooperation with each other, drew up the treaty in the Japanese, English, Dutch, and Chinese languages. All was ready at last for the final signing.

Accordingly, on Friday the 31st of March 1854, Commodore Matthew Calbraith Perry proceeded with all-necessary parade to the treaty house on shore just south of Yokohama, where, immediately on his arrival, he signed three drafts of the treaty written in the English language and delivered them to the commissioners, together with three copies of the same in the Dutch and Chinese languages certified by the interpreters, Messrs. Williams and Portman, for the United States of America. At the same instant, the Japanese commissioners, on behalf of the Empire of Japan, handed to the commodore three drafts of the treaty inscribed in the Japanese, Dutch, and Chinese languages, and signed by four of their number designated by the emperor for that purpose. A diplomatic triumph both for Matthew Perry and Japan's imperial commissioners, the Treaty of Kanagawa, as it became known, would prove to be an historic milestone for each country. Never again, whatever the future might bring, could the United States of America and Japan isolate themselves from each other.[21]

But surprise! To conclude Commodore Perry's

[21]Sewall, *Logbook,* pp. 239–62; Hawks, *Narrative of the Expedition*, Vol. I, pp. 343–77; Schroeder, "Perry," pp. 19–20; Dudden, *The American Pacific*, pp. 18–19.

drama successfully, a mysterious actor, Sewall confides, played a very important, yet concealed, role. Sewall's intriguing revelation emerged years later following conversations with Dr. Damon, a chaplain in Honolulu, when Sewall himself learned for the first time that an unseen friend of the United States aided the unknowing Americans in their negotiations. His name was Nakahama Manjiro, once a young shipwrecked Japanese fisherman rescued by an American whaler, who, for several years afterward in Massachusetts and elsewhere, learned English, among other useful skills, before he returned to Japan. In March 1854, Nakahama Manjiro, an officer by then in the Japanese Navy, was serving the commissioners dealing with Commodore Perry as their translator. "I was in a room adjoining that in which the negotiations were going on," Nakahama reportedly told Dr. Damon. "I was not allowed to see or communicate with any of the Americans. But each document from Commodore Perry I translated before it was handed to the commissioners, and the replies also I translated into English before they went to the commodore." This would explain why the American negotiators were mystified at the time, as the bargaining papers came to them not only in Dutch and Japanese but in English as well. Sewall realized that, "Nakahama was more than an interpreter. He knew the American people, the magnitude of their country, their wealth and commerce, their prestige and power. He believed in them. He was the channel through which by a kind of preordination American ideas filtered into Japan." If Dr. Damon's sensational story is true, Nakahama Manjiro behind the scenes must have greatly smoothed the task of the treaty makers. He must more than likely have reduced those misunderstandings and frictions invariably introduced by such disparate language and culture barriers as were present at Kanagawa on this extraordinary occasion.[22]

The Treaty of Kanagawa, in seeking to establish a "firm, lasting, and sincere friendship" between the United States and Japan, laid down in twelve Articles the rules to be mutually observed:

I. A fixed principle of "a perfect, permanent, and universal peace" without exception.

II. The ports of Shimoda and Hakodate granted by the Japanese for the reception of American ships, where such ships may obtain wood, water, provisions, coal, and other articles their needs may require.

III. Whenever ships of the United States are wrecked on the coast of Japan, the Japanese will aid them.

IV. Shipwrecked persons and other citizens of the United States shall be free as in other countries, and not subjected to confinement.

V. Shipwrecked men and other citizens of the United States, temporarily living at Shimoda

[22]Sewall, *Logbook*, pp. 243–44.

and Hakodate, shall be free to go where they please within prescribed limits of each place.

VI. If there be any other sort of goods wanted, or any business which shall require any special arrangements, there shall be careful deliberation between the parties to settle matters.

VII. United States vessels at the ports open to them may exchange gold and silver coin or articles of trade for other articles, and may carry away with them whatever articles they are unwilling to exchange.

VIII. Wood, water, provisions, coal, and goods shall only be procured through the agency of Japanese officers appointed for that purpose.

IX. If, at any future day, the government of Japan shall grant to any other nation or nations privileges and advantages not granted herein to the United States and its citizens, these same privileges shall be granted to the United States and its citizens without consultation or delay.

X. Ships of the United States shall be permitted to resort to no other ports in Japan but Shimoda and Hakodate, unless in distress or forced by stress of weather.

XI. The government of the United States shall appoint consuls or agents to reside in Shimoda at any time after the expiration of eighteen months from the date of signing this treaty, if either of the two governments deem such an arrangement necessary.

XII. Ratification of the treaty was to be exchanged within eighteen months, sooner if practicable.

Done at Kanagawa, the thirty-first day of March, in the year of our Lord Jesus Christ one thousand eight hundred and fifty-four, and of Kayei (that is *Keio*, the name of the Imperial reign) the seventh year, third month, and third day.[23]

Immediately, on signing and exchanging copies of the treaty, Commodore Perry presented the first commissioner, Prince Hayashi, with an American flag stating that this gift was the highest expression of national courtesy and friendship he could offer. The prince was deeply moved, and expressed his gratitude with evident feeling. The commodore next presented the other commissioners and the attending dignitaries with gifts he had especially reserved for them. All business now having been concluded to the satisfaction of both delegations, the Japanese commissioners invited Perry and his officers to enjoy a feast and entertainment especially prepared for the celebration.[24]

VIII

Commodore Perry entrusted the Treaty of Kanagawa to Commander Henry A. Adams, his Captain of the Fleet, for personal delivery to the government in Washington. Adams prepared at once to depart

[23]Hawks, *Narrative of the Expedition*, Vol. I, pp. 377–79.
[24]*Ibid.*, pp. 379–80.

aboard *Saratoga*, the ship longest in commission with the East India Squadron. On the fourth of April, with Adams as her passenger and the treaty as cargo, the *Saratoga*, in Captain's Clerk John Sewall's depiction, "spread her white wings for home," eastward bound for Honolulu four thousand miles across the Pacific Ocean. Getting underway, the *Saratoga* saluted the flag of the commodore with thirteen guns, which the *Powhatan* answered. "It was inspiring," Sewall remembered, "and to us who were at last homeward bound it was thrilling to hear the rousing cheers from each ship as we passed down the line, and from the commodore's band the strains of 'Home, Sweet Home.' " At Honolulu, Adams left the *Saratoga* to catch the very first ship leaving for San Francisco and another from there southward to Panama and the usual overland route across the isthmus, then he transshipped himself again to take the fourth and final passage of his long voyage home northward up the Atlantic Ocean. Completing his journey in three months and eight days, Commander Adams arrived in Washington on the 12th of July. And without delay, President Pierce submitted Perry's treaty to the Senate, which speedily and unanimously ratified it.

On September 30, Commander Adams sailed once more as a special courier bearing the ratified copy this time of the treaty for the Japanese. Adams sailed eastward from New York to England, next far to the south to round the nether tip of Africa for India, then he traveled overland across southern Asia to reach Hong Kong on New Year's Day 1855. Ready and waiting for him, U.S.S. *Powhatan* bore Adams to Japan. He arrived at Shimoda, January 26, embodying full powers himself as the appointed representative of the United States of America to exchange with Japan's authorities the ratifications of the treaty. Adams's return trip to Shimoda took him three months and twenty-seven days. Altogether, the elapsed time for his trip around the world between the signing of the treaty and its return to Japan, duly ratified by the president and Senate, was nine months and twenty-two days. The Treaty of Kanagawa inaugurating formal diplomatic ties for the United States and Japan, with the most-favored-nation principle embedded in Article IX, now became international law between them. The much-traveled Adams would hand Japan's ratified copy to Secretary of State W. L. Marcy in Washington on June 25, 1855.[25]

Following Adams's departure, Commodore Perry took parties of his officers and crewmen ashore for a much-needed change to tour their immediate surroundings. There was a great deal to pique their curiosities and catch their interests. Perry himself also enjoyed a leisurely stroll around Yokohama, where the seaport's mayor entertained him with

[25] *Ibid.*, Vol. I, pp. 393, 509; Vol. II, p. 210; Sewall, *Logbook*, pp. 259–60.

women and children present, an act of hospitality accorded no other foreigner before him for more than two centuries.

On April 9, Commodore Perry sent word over the protests of Japanese commissioners that he intended on the following day to order his two steamers as near to the city of Edo as the depth of the water would allow. (His third steam-powered frigate, U.S.S. *Susquehanna*, had been dispatched almost three weeks earlier to lend support to the United States Minister to China, who was caught up in the Taipings' turmoil.) Failing to dissuade Perry, the commissioners bade their frightened interpreters to stay on board to mark his movements. On Perry's orders, the steamships *Powhatan* and *Mississippi* impudently approached Edo's southern suburbs at their farthest reach. Through the mists, the commodore and the ships' lookouts could make out the immense city's thickly crowded streets, houses, and public buildings, along with low-lying profiles they assumed might conceal fortifications. The fears of the commissioners and interpreters for their own lives, seconded by the inexorable ebbing of the tide, persuaded Perry eventually to withdraw. "He thought it better not to bring about an issue that might endanger the very friendly position in which he had placed himself in relation to the Japanese. It would have been a source of endless regret, too, if to gratify a profitless curiosity, misfortune had been brought upon the commissioners, whose

Street in Hakodate; from The Expedition of an American Squadron

Courtesy The Beverly R. Robinson Collection, United States Naval Academy Museum, Annapolis, Maryland

friendly conduct deserved every kind return that might be given in consonance with duty."

The warships, as the result, returned to their "American anchorage." The Japanese interpreters, who remained on board during the entire trip, felt enormously relieved, and soon "they participated with the greatest conviviality in a collation which was spread for their entertainment in the commodore's cabin."

Not needing to remain any longer in the upper part of the Bay of Edo, the squadron backed down to Shimoda for a lengthier examination of the seaport's surroundings. Perry's pleasure became evident. The harbor at Shimoda was superb for a limited number of ships, convenient to the open sea, without any peculiar problems whatever for shiphandlers. "I do not see," said Perry, "how a more desirable port could have been selected to answer all the purposes for which it is wanted." Then Perry's flotilla left Japan's principal island of Honshu altogether, to travel northeastward to Hakodate, the other treaty port, which was located on the south coast of Esso, or Yesso, as the island, later renamed Hokkaido, was sometimes transliterated in that period. Remote and outlying, Hakodate was a struggling town of about a thousand houses and little else. All on board the American ships who had ever called at Gibraltar were struck by Hakodate's resemblance to that mighty fortification. There was the same lonely outcropping of rock with the town's houses gathered at its base, and the shallow neck of land reaching toward higher ground beyond, the capacious bay, and the narrow channel separating the two mainlands, the islands of Honshu and Hokkaido–like the straits between the Atlantic Ocean and the Mediterranean Sea that divide Europe from North Africa. The commodore and his senior officers were welcomed inside some of Hakodate's homes. This remote seaport would serve its purposes perfectly well as a place of refuge, but little else could be certified in its favor.[26]

At the end of June 1854, Commodore Perry ushered his squadron's remaining ships out of Japanese waters for the last time. His skillful diplomacy had won the treaty he sought to open up Japan, and his ambitions for an American commercial empire in the far western Pacific were coming sharply into focus. His expedition's investigations of Lew Chew and the Bonin Islands, for example, convinced him that the United States ought to take them over. As a first step, Perry returned directly to Naha, and quickly signed a treaty of friendship with Japan's regent there. He recommended, in due course, that the United States should install a colony on the island of Taiwan (later to be named Formosa under Japan's control) at the port of Kelung. Besides the

[26]Hawks, *Narrative of the Expedition*, Vol. I, pp. 394–95, 398–99, 401, 491; Samuel Eliot Morison, "Introduction," *The Japan Expedition, 1852–1854: the Personal Journal of Commodore Matthew C. Perry,* edited by Roger Pineau (Washington: Smithsonian Institution Press, 1968), pp. xviii–xix.

Commodore Perry Paying His Farewell Visit to the Imperial Commissioners at Shimoda; from The Expedition of an American Squadron

Courtesy The Beverly R. Robinson Collection, United States Naval Academy Museum, Annapolis, Maryland

rich coal deposits on Taiwan, an American settlement under national auspices could foster trading with Asia's mainland countries. It would fix a handy location to construct naval and military bases for overseeing the principal seaports of China and in time might be expected to rival Singapore and Hong Kong for its commercial importance. Perry's strategic conception of an American Pacific empire far outdistanced the thinking of his contemporaries. By nearly four decades, he anticipated the vision of Alfred Thayer Mahan, the greatest strategist of the United States Navy and the influential author of books highlighting the significance of sea power in history. For now, however, Matthew Perry was a weary man, worn out by the constant anxieties, his health visibly debilitated. He temporarily relinquished the command of his East India Squadron in September to head home to a well-deserved leave and a hero's welcome.

Back at Shimoda before much longer, on returning to exchange ratifications of the Treaty of Kanagawa, Commander Adams had found to his dismay "a great and sad change" in the seaport and its environs from an earthquake's devastation of December 23, 1854. Major shocks were felt along the whole of Japan's coastline doing some injury to Edo, severely damaging Shimoda, and entirely destroying Osaka. Every house and public building on the low grounds surrounding Shimoda's waterfront had collapsed. All that escaped were a few temples, shrines, and private structures on elevated land. Only sixteen edifices remained of what was once the heart of Shimoda's village community. Nevertheless, the imperial commissioners were awaiting Adams to exchange ratifications.

A couple of technical objections arose. The first difficulty stemming from the treaty's diverse translations was easily resolved. One version specified that the treaty must be ratified *within* eighteen months, while the other stated *after* eighteen months. Quickly, the two parties agreed to drop the matter altogether as insignificant. More serious, a second objection raised by Adams concerned the signatures affixed to the treaty. Whereas both President Pierce and Secretary of State Marcy had already signed their names, the Americans insisted that the Emperor of Japan must sign as well, not merely his supreme councillors. After some confusion and hesitation among the Japanese, in having to depart from the ancient precedent for keeping the sovereign aloof from mundane business, this was done. Finally, with agreement reached and all obstacles removed, the imperial commissioners, in genuine concern, inquired earnestly about Commodore Perry's health. Expressing generous sentiments of both friendship and remembrance, they charged Adams to assure Perry that "his name would live forever in the history of Japan." And today's visitors to the lovely resort of Shimoda will still find a bust of Matthew Calbraith Perry facing

View of Shimoda from the American Graveyard; from The Expedition of an American Squadron

Courtesy The Beverly R. Robinson Collection, United States Naval Academy Museum, Annapolis, Maryland

the harbor as well as a monument on the heights overhead commemorating his role in the opening of Japan. Even the savagery of the Great Pacific War of 1941–45 and the humiliation of the Allied occupation have failed to tarnish his accomplishment.

Congress voted the country's appreciation to Commodore Perry, for his services as special ambassador to Japan and commander of the naval expedition, with a grant of $20,000 to publish the three-volume *Narrative of the Expedition*. Gifts showered on him included a gigantic silver service from New York's Chamber of Commerce, and a large silver salver presented by the governor and General Assembly of Rhode Island, his native state. His vitality apparently recovered, Matthew Perry was being touted to take command of the prestigious Mediterranean Squadron, when, in early 1858, he succumbed to a dangerous cold, sickened dramatically, and, in March, he died.

In 1859, John Smith Sewall was ordained as a Congregational minister and installed as the pastor in Wenham, Massachusetts, a pulpit he held until 1867. Sewall thereafter pursued an academic career as a professor, first at Bowdoin College, his *alma mater*, next, until retirement, at Bangor Theological Seminary.

More than eighty years old when he died in 1911, Sewall had published some half-dozen books, as well as essays on theology, history, and biography. Over the years, John Sewall's fascination with various developments throughout Asia, never did flag.[27]

IX

In truth, it was Townsend Harris, the first United States consul general, who effectively opened the door to Japan. Appointed in 1855, Harris arrived in Shimoda the next year, the first American envoy under the new Treaty of Kanagawa. Commodore Perry had, of course, initiated Japan into Western-style diplomatic and commercial relations with the United States, but his treaty, notwithstanding its highly prized most-favored-nation clause, included no guarantee for commencing trade. Harris, a Columbia College alumnus and Manhattan merchant, had served as president of New York City's Board of Education, and helped to acquire the charter for establishing the present City College of New York, now a division of City University. On July 29, 1858, having just arranged a commercial treaty between the United States and Siam (Thailand), Townsend Harris skillfully and patiently concluded a new pact with Japan establishing formal diplomatic relations with the United States. Under the new agreement, Japan opened the ports of Nagasaki and Kanagawa while approving freedom of trade as a guiding principle and a schedule of import tariffs.

[27]Hawks, *Narrative of the Expedition*, Vol. I, pp. 508–13; Sewall, *Logbook*, pp. 229–31; Schroeder, "Perry," pp. 20–23; for Sewall, see *Who Was Who in America*, 1897–1942, Vol. I, p. 1105.

First Japanese Ministers to the United States

Courtesy National Archives, College Park, Maryland

Quickly the British, French, Russians, and Dutch secured equivalent treaties for themselves; Japan was pressed by these four powers to fix even lower import duties and concede rights of extraterritoriality for foreign nationals. These provisions were duplicated in pacts with other nations, and extended far and wide through the most-favored-nation principle. In 1859, Townsend Harris was elevated to the ambassadorial rank of minister and inaugurated the first U.S. legation in Edo.[28]

In the following year of 1860, Japan's first diplomatic delegation traveled to the United States aboard U.S.S. *Powhatan*, to exchange in Washington the ratifications of Harris's treaty and install Nippon's first legation. An interest in acquiring Western technology at once became most evident. Japan's intensely patriotic warrior nobles, young *samurai*, feared for their own nation a national degradation from Western inroads like China's. To build up Japan's military and economic strength, they chose the road to modernization, and drove themselves in self-protection to challenge the time-worn shogunate's feudal government. In June, seventy or so Japanese dignitaries and their attendants traveled by train from Washington to Philadelphia eager to inspect the Quaker City's industries, most

[28]William Elliott Griffis, *Townsend Harris: First American Envoy to Japan* (Boston and New York: Houghton, Mifflin, 1895), *passim*; Mario Emilio Cosenza, *The Complete Journal of Townsend Harris*, 2d ed. (Rutland,VT: C.E. Tuttle, 1959), *passim*; Dudden, *The American Pacific*, pp. 136–37.

especially the United States Mint. Although the Civil War, as well as Reconstruction, 1861–77, would forestall for many years any further adventuring by the United States into the western Pacific, the Japanese pushed ahead unabatingly to repudiate their isolated past. The seaport cities of Niigata and Hyogo (Kobe) opened for commerce between 1860 and 1863, with Edo and Osaka newly made available for foreign residences. In 1876 for the Centennial Exposition, a Japanese delegation came back to Philadelphia for a second official visit, this time proudly to display its nation's many accomplishments. In fact, Japan's shogunate had been overthrown a decade earlier.

By the imperial restoration of 1867, fifteen-year-old Mutsuhito became the Mikado, the highest authority in Japan. He took for himself the name of Emperor Meiji in 1869, and he moved the court from Kyoto to Edo, renaming the city Tokyo, "eastern capital."

In Emperor Meiji's name, Japan modernized itself within a generation, surging forward to dismantle almost overnight the seven-centuries-old feudal structures, attempting to overtake the West to make up for the nation's lengthy isolation. Emperor Meiji's Charter Oath of April 1868 singled out "evil customs of the past" to be terminated, with knowledge to be sought everywhere, "so as to strengthen the foundations of imperial rule." Eager young men journeyed off to England, Germany,

France, and the United States to learn all they could about modern technology. "The world was one vast schoolhouse for them," as noted by Edwin O. Reischauer. "Students were carefully chosen on the basis of their knowledge and capabilities, and the countries where they were to study were selected with equal care.

"The Japanese determined to learn from each Western country that in which it particularly excelled." Great Britain's navy and parliament, for example, served as models for the Japanese, as did the armies of France and Prussia. American postal, agricultural, as well as educational technicians were brought into Japan to instruct eager modernizers.

At breathtaking speed, Japan's leaders proceeded to transform their society into an industrialized, militarized, and highly nationalistic civilization. Its diplomats, throughout both the 1870s and 1880s, strove to overturn the one-sided treaties imposed on Japan by the Western powers, which patronizingly implied the racial inferiority of the Japanese people, confined their economy, and, in numerous ways, hobbled the nation's sovereignty. To inhibit any Japanese propositions for modifying either the foreigners' extraterritorial rights or the inequitable schedules of tariffs, unanimity of agreement had to be reached among the powers, who invariably attempted to exchange any concessions they might have to yield for complete, unfettered accessibility to Japan's markets and people. When Great

Britain relinquished her rights of extraterritoriality in Japan in 1894, the United States followed suit, but Washington reserved the right to restrict Japanese immigration.[29]

X

China was a different matter. Somehow, following the Taiping Rebellion, China's Ch'ing Dynasty managed to make China's archaic system work by adopting a limited number of Western ways. Driven by co-regent Prince Kung, China temporarily stymied the possibilities of foreign intervention or internal revolution. The self-strengthening movement was the imperial court's long-term defensive program. Unfortunately, self-strengthening restricted itself to equipping China with weapons, ships, machines, mines, communications, and light manufactures. China during this period never attained an industrial takeoff point, as the defeats Peking suffered in wars with France, 1884–85, and Japan, a decade later, so demonstrated. Western philosophy, culture, and the arts were spurned as being too barbarian. Steadfast, if viewed from within, the

[29]Edwin O. Reischauer, *Japan: the Story of a Nation*, rev. ed. (New York: Alfred A. Knopf, 1974), pp. 3–144; Scott F. Runkle, *An Introduction to Japanese History* (Tokyo: International Society for Educational Information Press, 1976), pp. 23–27; also Russell F. Weigley, ed. *Philadelphia: a 300-Year History* (New York: W. W. Norton, 1982), pp. 381–82, 466–70; Charles E. Neu, *The Troubled Encounter: the United States and Japan* (New York: John Wiley & Sons, 1975), pp. 25–27.

Celestial Empire remained the center of civilization.

In 1868, Prince Kung appointed Anson Burlingame, the retiring United States ambassador, to head a diplomatic mission intended to discourage the Europeans and Americans from hurrying the modernization process for China. In California, accompanied by Manchu and Chinese co-envoys, Burlingame grandly proclaimed that China was prepared at last to welcome "the shining banners of Western civilization." In New York City, he announced missionaries would be permitted "to plant the shining cross on every hill and every valley."

The Burlingame Treaty, which he negotiated in Washington, bound the United States to noninterference in Chinese affairs, and provided for the entry of Chinese consuls and laborers into the United States, with reciprocal rights for Americans in China of residence, religion, travel, and education. Among the treaty's effects, some 120 long-gowned boys, sponsored in four installments by the Chinese Educational Mission, lived with host families in the Connecticut Valley, 1872–81, attended schools, and learned to play baseball before the experiment was aborted by conservative opponents from both sides. Racist agitation was spreading against the more than one hundred thousand Chinese workers already in the United States, and even acts of brutality grew commonplace. Pressures increased to exclude any new immigrants, a stand which both major political parties supported in their platforms of 1880. The United States government forced a treaty revision on China to allow the suspension of Chinese immigration, though not its prohibition, and Congress promptly enacted such an interruption for a period of ten years–the initial step toward the eventual policy, in 1904, of permanent exclusion.

Meanwhile, the self-strengthening movement was faltering. Mandarins maintained their traditional disdain for merchants and industrialists, while scholars covertly directed the imperial court's foot-dragging against modernization. Reactionary resistance often expressed itself in anti-Christian outbursts. Claims of Taipings and other rebels to be Christians did not help, nor did the Christian practice of males and females worshipping together in mixed assemblies. Chinese converts too frequently displayed a blatant intolerance for ancient beliefs and time-honored customs. They seemed to cast aside all respect for elders by refusing to pay homage to ancestors. If afoul of the law, they knew that missionaries would come to their aid. Not only were China's modernizers distracted, but vital resources drained away from the self-strengthening effort. A scramble for concessions by the foreign powers was threatening to divide up China, much as like Africa's recent partitioning into three colonies–British, French, and German.

With the outbreak of the Spanish-American War, Commodore George Dewey hurriedly drove his flotilla from Hong Kong down the South China Sea to sink Spain's fleet, May 1, 1898, at its moorings in Manila Bay. Control of the Philippine Islands moved the United States forcibly onto China's threshold. Not only was the United States becoming a great power in East Asia in its own right, it now held a nearby sphere of influence over China's external affairs.

During the same time, China's Ch'ing dynasty (1644–1912) was fast expiring and threatening, by its impending demise, to extinguish the oldest empire on earth. Floods in Shantung and droughts in northern China added famine on a vast scale to the sufferings of the populace. Victims spread the superstition that their ancestral gods were punishing the Chinese people for the terrible wrongdoings of the foreigners in the nation's midst. Secret antiforeign and anti-Christian societies proliferated. The Society of Righteous and Harmonious Fists, its members known by the nickname of the "Boxers," was one such clandestine organization, especially influential among frustrated army officers. Rampaging and pillaging across northern China during the summer months of 1900, the Boxers, some 140,000 strong, murdered scores of Christian missionaries and thousands of Chinese converts, then besieged the diplomatic legations in the city of Peking where they put to death a Japanese envoy, as well as the ambassador from Germany.

The Boxer Rebellion brought about a dramatic

retaliation from the foreign powers and left behind an enduring residue. President William McKinley ordered twenty-five hundred American troops from the Philippines to join the international relief expedition of soldiers, sailors, and marines being assembled by eight nations. Secretary of State John Hay, in his definitive Open Door note of July 3, 1900, laid down United States policy as seeking to guarantee: 1) the protection of American lives and property; 2) the opportunity for open and impartial trading; and 3) the integrity of China's territory and sovereignty. In sum, Hay's policy was a determination by the United States for keeping China intact in the face of foreign threats and the trading door open. The military relief expedition crushed the Boxers by force, and rescued the trapped diplomats and their families from the beleaguered legations. McKinley countermanded the subsequent orders he had issued directing a ten thousand-man American force to China, and transferred to the Philippines two-thirds of the sixty-three hundred men already there. Foreign troops were authorized to remain in Peking to protect their legations, and to station themselves at various intermediate places between the capital and the seaports. Inasmuch as governmental reforms following the uprising came grudgingly, far too little and much too late, the prestige of the Celestial Empire sank visibly lower and lower. More Chinese hearkened to the republican appeal of the revolutionary Dr. Sun Yat-sen.

Although fragile and insubstantial, the United States's Open Door Policy for China commenced before long to carry considerable weight. The Open Door Policy could not invariably succeed, of course, but, like the Monroe Doctrine, it would lodge itself in the public mind at home as the morally righteous and patriotic course for American foreign relations to take in East Asia.

In 1904, when the Immigration Act of that year barred permanently the entry of any more Chinese, the United States fixed the strength of its legation guard in Peking at 305 soldiers and marines. For emergency service in China, a force of 2,000 soldiers stationed in the Philippines was specifically designated, a unit that could expand to 5,000 men if need be.

An American infantry battalion moved into barracks at Tientsin following the revolution of 1911, followed by a second battalion in 1914 to protect access routes to Peking. The United States Navy's Asiatic Squadron by then had grown to forty-eight vessels, including one battleship, two armored cruisers, numerous gunboats and utility craft. This sizable fleet was standing by, the government in Washington proclaimed, to insure "the interests of civilization and trade" and to deliver, if called upon, "severe and lasting punishment" to any agency foolhardy enough to threaten the safety of Americans anywhere in East Asia. As President

Theodore Roosevelt explained the situation, "our future history will be more determined by our position on the Pacific facing China than by our position on the Atlantic facing Europe."[30]

XI

Unfortunately, Japan's efforts to redress her unequal treaties with the Western powers coincided with these fresh waves of imperialism. In 1867, in fact, the United States had expanded its sovereignty far westward by purchasing Alaska from Russia, and picking up Midway Island. Japan commenced to imitate the strong-arm methods of the great powers, if only to gain parity with them in China. Jurisdictional disputes broke out after 1871 between Japan and China over their conflicting interests in the Lew Chew Islands, in Taiwan, and in Korea. China was rapidly losing influence in these ancient tributary areas, while Japan, intruding into the opportunities at hand, avidly prospected for food, raw materials, markets, and strategic sites for military bases. Japan annexed the Lew Chew Islands in 1879, renaming them the Ryukyu Islands. In Tokyo, leaders endeavored next to turn hapless Korea into a thoroughfare to Manchuria against czarist Russia's rival ambitions.

The Korean peninsula lay athwart Japan's direct

[30]Hsü, *The Rise of Modern China*, pp. 259–439; Dudden, *The American Pacific*, pp. 82–90, 112–21.

route to Manchuria's rich resources and Japan's exploitative goals for China. After Japan trounced China in the First Sino-Japanese War, from 1894–95, Korea for a brief decade became nominally independent, while Japan then obtained sovereignty over Taiwan, renamed Formosa, and acquired the Pescadores Islands off Formosa's west coast. Few Americans at this stage spoke out to oppose Japan's surprising expansion at China's expense. The Japanese victory even won scattered applause from a number of Americans, being viewed as additional evidence of their Asian *protégé*'s enlightened progress.

More disturbing, though, were Japan's next steps. Japan defeated Russia in their war of 1904–05 and went on, between 1905 and 1910, formally to annex Korea, the "Land of Morning Calm," renaming that ancient kingdom Chosen and absorbing the Koreans into Japan's burgeoning empire. The Japanese had learned their lessons well. Western powers now treated Japan with respect.

Inexorably, the paths pursued by Japan and the United States were converging. Trouble surfaced over the Hawaiian Islands even before their annexation, where an oligarchy of Americans, who had overthrown the native monarchy, ruled a polyglot republic including thousands of Japanese sugar cane laborers, while the United States Navy developed its mid-Pacific base at Pearl Harbor. Rumors that Japan was scheming to invade these islands inflamed debates between the annexationists and anti-imperialists, who for obviously selfish motives were supported by sugar beet interests on the mainland. During the Spanish-American War of 1898, Congress by joint resolution annexed the Hawaiian Islands, and next, by the treaty of peace, the United States acquired the Philippine Islands from Spain, together with Guam and Wake islands, to launch thereby a fullblown imperial rivalry in the western Pacific between Japan and the United States. In 1899, in additional proof of Manifest Destiny's seaworthiness, the United States obtained sovereignty over the six easternmost Samoan Islands. Japanese anxieties, touched off by the development of the Pearl Harbor naval base at Honolulu, became secondary from this point to alarms over the United States's steps to fortify the Philippine Islands. Southeast of Japan, the archipelago lay at China's doorstep and close to the East Indies. East Asia's balance of power would be at issue from this moment forward.[31]

At first, Theodore Roosevelt applauded Japan's spectacular victory over Russia, since the czar's despotism was everywhere unpopular, until he recognized the dangers inherent in its magnitude. Probably a Russian victory, if the outcome had

[31]Neu, *The Troubled Encounter*, pp. 25–30; Reischauer, *Japan*, pp. 116–51; Runkle, *Japanese History*, p. 26; Wei Peh T'i, East Asian History, 1870–1952 (Hong Kong: Oxford University Press, 1981), pp. 29–30; Dudden, *The American Pacific*, pp. 22–24, 48, 65–66, 142–45.

been reversed, would have excluded Americans from doing business in Manchuria, given Russia's insistent demands on China for a commercial monopoly. But, more worrisome, it was becoming plausible that Japan's victorious generals and admirals might one day challenge the Open Door Policy. It might be better, as President Roosevelt was beginning to see things, if Russia and Japan were to compete face to face in open rivalry to moderate each other's imperial ambitions. Softening his support for the Open Door, Roosevelt evenhandedly conceded Japan's priority in Korea in return for Japan's acceptance of American dominion in the Philippines, yet he turned China's anger at the Japanese against himself in the process. Undaunted, Roosevelt seized the opportunity to mediate the settlement of the Russo-Japanese War (1904–05). He called together the triumphant but exhausted Japanese and the defeated Russians for peace talks, August 1905, at the naval base in Portsmouth, New Hampshire, and proceeded ebulliently to win a Nobel Peace Prize for himself by settling their conflict. Japan went ahead, this time unchallenged, to absorb Korea outright over the next five years, as well as virtually to freeze out American merchants and investors altogether from Korea and Manchuria.

Thereafter to 1941, relations between the United States and Japan evolved, almost exclusively, around the problems posed by American racial hostility against Orientals and the rivalry of the two countries to determine China's future. When, in 1904, about fifteen thousand Japanese entered the United States, many of them through the Hawaiian Islands, Californians shrieked out their alarm. Anti-Japanese and anti-Korean immigration leagues sprang up. California's governor denounced the "Japanese menace," and the legislature debated barring any more Orientals from entering the state. In San Francisco, in 1906, the Board of Education established a segregated Oriental School for the city's Chinese, Japanese, and Korean boys and girls touching off an international crisis in the face of Tokyo's angry protests. Rioting burst out against Asians all along the West Coast from Los Angeles to Vancouver. Carefully, to dampen the hysteria, President Roosevelt persuaded Congress to prohibit Japanese immigration from Hawaii to the mainland. He also approved a "Gentlemen's Agreement" in March 1907, whereby Tokyo promised to halt the emigration of laborers to the United States, while Washington promised to take steps to prevent discrimination against the nation's residents of Japanese background.

In 1908, in a show of strength, President Roosevelt ordered the navy's entire complement of sixteen battleships to embark on a goodwill cruise across the Pacific Ocean and around the world. At Yokohama, Japan greeted America's "Great White Fleet," where a rousing reception for the crews featured rows upon rows of schoolchildren waving American flags and attempting to sing "The Star-Spangled Banner." The two governments promised to respect each other's possessions and maintain the status quo in the Pacific region, also to uphold the independence and integrity of China in keeping with the Open Door principle of equal opportunity for the commerce and industry of all nations. Roosevelt then emphasized the peaceful intent of America's relations with Japan, and the emperor's emissaries declared that Japan had never even contemplated making war against the United States. The tenor of these exchanges pleased President Roosevelt. The future seemed secure in March 1909, when he left office just after the Great White Fleet returned home.[32]

Arthur Power Dudden

Bryn Mawr College
June 1995

[32]Dudden, *The American Pacific*, pp. 83, 145–63.

The Logbook of the Captain's Clerk

Adventures in the China Seas

Author's Prefatory

It is now half a century since the "opening" of Japan. That famous document—the treaty negotiated by Commodore Matthew Calbraith Perry—was completed and signed on the thirty-first day of March in 1854. All the signers are now dead and gone. So are nearly all the actors in the great expedition. As I stand by the half-century milestone and look back in quest of the two thousand officers and men who accompanied the American envoy to the Empire of the Rising Sun, it has a sobering effect to find that less than a score of them are known to be living. I feel as if I were alone with my memories, a survivor of a vanished epoch of history.

These pages contain the record of our principal adventures in those distant seas. I can hardly assume that they should have any special interest for any but personal friends. And yet, apart from the excitement of mere adventure, the testimony of an eyewitness to the scenes and events of the Japan expedition, and to some of the curious phenomena of the Taiping Rebellion, might seem to claim a kind of historical value. Japan has more recently startled nations with the rapidity of her growth, with the brilliant efflorescence of her new civilization. It is instructive to look back half a century and study the contrast.

In their original form some of these narratives first saw the light in the pages of various magazines. I owe my thanks to the proprietors of the *New Englander*, the *Century*, and the *Forest and Stream*, for their courteous permission to use material which they had published before. I should be glad to express my obligations to the *Knickerbocker* also; but that delightful old monthly has long since passed within the shade.

I let this little book go out into the wide, wide world with a feeling of affectionate regret. It was my fortune for the next four years after college to "follow the sea"; and ever since then the sea has followed me—haunted me with its visions, with its memories, with its infinite suggestions of stress and peril, of melancholy and music, of gallant life and lurking death. It has been for many years the recreation of a busy life to call up these distant scenes and reincarnate them in monographs for the entertainment of friends. And now that I gather them and clothe them with the dignity of a book, and as the little volume goes out of its nest in my heart into the chilly atmosphere of the world, I experience something of the sentiment one feels in sparing a favorite child who leaves the fireside for some unknown and distant home.

If it should chance to reach any of the survivors of the memorable expedition, let it carry a warm

Commodore Matthew Calbraith Perry
After His Return from Japan
Photograph by Matthew Brady; Courtesy Library of Congress

greeting from an old comrade. Nearly all of our shipmates have finished their voyage. And for us who remain, who have faced so many perils of storm and wreck, and for whom the sun must be now far down the western sky, the poet's prayer appeals to our sailor instinct as well as to our aspirations for the immortal life:

Sunset and evening star,
And one clear call for me!
And may there be no moaning of the bar
When I put out to sea;

But such a tide as moving seems asleep,
Too full for noise and foam,
When that which drew from out the boundless deep
Turns again home.

Twilight and evening bell,
And after that the dark!
And may there be no sadness of farewell
When I embark.

For though from out our bourne of Time and Place
The flood may bear me far,
I hope to see my Pilot face to face
When I have crossed the bar.*

JOHN S. SEWALL

1905

*Alfred, Lord Tennyson (1809–92), "Crossing the Bar." Not the last poem written by Tennyson, though written in his eighty-first year; it appears at his request as the final poem in all collections of his work.—Ed.

I

On the Way Out

TO THE NOVICE on the deck of a man-of-war, everything is strange and some things are startling. Having thus far wended his way through life as a landlubber, the transition to ship, sea, sailors, and storms is somewhat bewildering. It takes time to learn the names and uses of the tangled tracery around him. And when at last he can discriminate between the mizzen to' gallant brace and the foretopmast stun'sail halliard, he can be credited with a brave beginning. The big guns, portholes, armchests, cutlass racks, carbines, boarding pikes, and other belligerent contrivances suggest a martial contrast to the peaceful atmosphere of his former life on shore. And the tipsy deck, swelling canvas, and webs of cordage strike him as quite unlike the solid old home of his boyhood, which staid where it was put and never threatened to spill him out. Our craft was an old-timer; not a modern gunboat nor an armored cruiser; but an old-fashioned sloop of war, a full-rigged ship, equipped with a ponderous battery of twenty-two guns—eighteen thirty-twos and four sixty-eights; no modern languid luxuries; no new-fangled aids of electricity; in fact we went equipped with lightning conductors on fore and main masts on purpose to ward off all such electricity as we might happen to encounter; no steam, save that which ascended in fragrant incense from the ship's coppers.

Her driving force came from no such common and profane thing as steam, engendered in iron boilers and set as a slave to drive pistons and turn cranks; but from the sweet free winds of heaven that played upon her sails and swelled them into curves of beauty. She was a handsome craft; and when clothed in snowy white from deck to royal masthead, bending before the blast and driving on over the green seas and through the sparkling foam, she made a superb picture that even a landsman would admire. Her complement counted up to 210—a total of 22 officers and 188 in the crew.

My place was that of the captain's clerk;* a youngster just out of college, serving Uncle Sam presumably from patriotism, but mainly with an eye to Uncle Sam's gold to pay off college debts. In close relations with a good-natured commander, the clerk may have great advantages of observation; accordingly, the chronicles of adventure set forth in these pages are the testimony of an eyewitness to the principal scenes described.

*A "clerk" in the United States Navy at that time was neither a commissioned nor a warrant officer; neither an enlisted rating nor a sailor. The commodore or captain chose his own clerk, and could dismiss him at his pleasure. Robert H. Rankin, *Uniforms of the Sea Services: a Pictorial History* (Annapolis, MD: United States Naval Institute, 1962), p. 46.—Ed.

We got underway from Hampton Roads* in September 1850, bound for the underside of the world. We were to relieve the *St. Mary's* or some other long-absent member of our squadron in the East Indies and then stay as long ourselves. In the end it proved much longer. Before night of the first day out we had sunk the capes of the Chesapeake and left the whole broadside of the continent hull down on the western horizon. Alone on the sea and "visited all night by troops of stars." It may not be worth philosophizing about, but to this day solemn strains of music will always call up the vision of a ship setting forth alone on the long journey over the infinite waste, sailing out from the protecting homeland into the mysterious future, knowing well that she is to run the gauntlet of reefs and shoals and storms, but not knowing whether she will bear herself bravely through all perils and proudly return, or will end her voyage and her life in the depths of the sea.

There is melody in the accompaniments of the voyage itself; the piping and twittering of soft airs through the rigging, the tinkle of silver ripples lapping the bows, the drowsy hum of the men at their work, the rat-ta-tattoo of the reef-points on the

*Hampton Roads, Virginia, one of the finest natural anchorages in the world, has long been important for the United States Navy. The James, Nansemond, and Elizabeth rivers pass there into Chesapeake Bay. Newport News and Hampton are on the north shore, with Norfolk and Portsmouth on the south. —Ed.

topsails, the shrill blasts of the gale, the keen fife notes of the boatswain's whistle, the answering shouts from aloft, the roaring diapason of the waves, the swash and crackle and thunder of great watery masses sweeping in over the bulwarks or rushing aft into the seething wake—these sounds of the sea make a rough symphony that will at any moment set the blood tingling in a sailor's veins. It may be that the echoes of that noisy life now far receding still send through the chambers of memory their faint throbbing pulsations of sound. Or it may be that the music of it all is only a touch of remembered sentiment. That far-away past was luminous then with the hopes of youth and the promise of adventure; it is hallowed now with memories of a life that is vanished and of friends who are gone.

Alone on the sea, yet not in absolute solitude, for we had a welcome from shoals of porpoises that gambolled around, flying fish that skittered along the crests of the waves, an occasional surly shark, and flocks of gulls and petrels that made the welkin lively with their curvettings and chatterings. Our voyage was a kind of royal progress, attended by a nimble retinue of the denizens of the deep, all animated by the same tender interest in whatever savory morsels might be thrown overboard by the mess cooks and left floating in our wake.

The first thing was to make sufficient easting and so catch the trades; whose genial gales sent us bowling down the Atlantic and well into the peaceful tropical main that Spanish sailors used to call *el golfo de las damas*—the ladies' sea—because in those gentle waters one could entrust the helm to a young girl without danger. Of course we met Neptune, trident and all. We were honored with a visit from his briny majesty when we crossed the line, and our fresh-water sailors who had never crossed before were duly initiated by his aqueous myrmidons. Below the line the southeast trades swept us smoothly along into the magnificent bay of Rio de Janeiro. There we exchanged naval courtesies with the frigates *Congress* and *Raritan*; bustled around the city on tours of observation, or on shopping and foraging trips; went to the opera to see their majesties the emperor and empress of Brazil; climbed the peak of Corcovado; and then, freighted with sweet memories of tropical scenery and luscious fruit, cut across the Atlantic to the rocky and sandy contrasts of South Africa. Our first port was Saldanha Bay, some twenty leagues north of Cape Town; a superb landlocked basin, and, like the great bay of Rio, well worthy of its fame as one of the finest natural harbors in the world. Sweeping in from the tumbling ocean outside, you find yourself floating on a broad and deep estuary like a placid lake that reaches some twenty miles in among the hills. When we entered, it was deserted and still; not a hut nor a tree in sight; the low brown sandy hills overspread with brush; the waters dappled with swarms of wildfowl that appeared in fluttering clouds from the sea. But

Saldanha Bay itself had not always been a solitude.

Two centuries ago Saldanha Bay was a busy half-way station for the great convoys of merchantmen that called here to rest and recruit on their way to the distant east; and more than once it thundered and smoked with terrific battles between Dutch and English squadrons that here hunted each other to the death. They were contending for the primacy of the Cape; a bloody prelude to the more recent struggles in the Transvaal.* All this has now faded into the dim past. The great harbor bears again the peaceful messengers of commerce, and its shores are alive with a thrifty population whose broad wheat farms mantle the hills and valleys with gold. In a mild way some of us youngsters woke again the echoes of war, trying it on the springbok, the beautiful little "gazelle of the south," which ever and anon darted up from our path. But the dear creatures were too nimble for us and bolted over and under the brush with such lightning speed that by the time we could bring our clumsy muskets to bear where they were, they were somewhere else.

Cape Town readily furnished us the supplies that Saldanha Bay could not. Ten days of town life under the lee of Table Mountain made a comfortable prologue to the blustering Cape of Good Hope—

*Sewall refers to the bitter warfare for dominion between the Dutch Boers and Britain's imperial forces. The Cape of Good Hope lies at the tip of South Africa. The Transvaal is South Africa's northeastern republic, and Johannesburg is its largest city.—Ed.

Cape Town and Table Mountain; from The Expedition of an American Squadron

Courtesy The Beverly R. Robinson Collection, United States Naval Academy Museum, Annapolis, Maryland

much more accurately described by its original title, the Cape of Storms. We did not run down to the "roaring forties" to get by, though one would think so from the fury and foam; for a tearing gale drove us around and gave us a vigorous shove up the Indian Ocean. Sixty days more of sunshine and storm brought us to our next halting place, a Malay island on the northern edge of the Banda Sea. This was Bouro, one of the Spice Islands.* The port was Cajelie Bay—rechristened by our irreverent tars Catch-helly Bay, because we drove into it before a furious rain-squall that nearly piled us on a reef before we could get our anchor down. A beautiful spot, rich with tropical verdure, mountainous, balmy, aromatic. In size it is just one third as large as the state of Vermont; and as some of its peaks rise to a height of more than eight thousand feet, the scenery is superb. We found there a solitary European, the Dutch Resident,** deputy and factor of the power that holds so many of those fertile gardens of the east; around him, Malay tribes who occupy the seacoast rim of the island, while the interior is tenanted by those mysterious aborigines, the Alfuras. Our business in this small paradise was to wood and water the ship. And while that task was going forward, other incidents happened that

*Mountainous, fertile, and very humid, the Spice Islands, known today as Indonesia's Moluccas, were the original home of nutmeg and cloves.—Ed.

**A provincial official of the Netherlands (Dutch) East Indies.—Ed.

helped to keep up the supply of ozone in the atmosphere of the steerage.

Did you ever buy potatoes from a king? If not, try Bouro; you will find it as easy as forming a trust or selling a mine. One morning a brace of port steerage youngsters landed and sallied into the village in quest of plantains, yams, fruit, or anything legitimately edible in our somewhat fastidious mess. For legal tender we carried fresh from the purser's storeroom a new jackknife and a bright tin pan. Sauntering along the street we came upon one enclosure that seemed larger and more tidy than the rest, in which a few natives were lolling at their ease. They rose and graciously welcomed us in. We made known our errand by signs; whereupon the venerable proprietor took our basket and filled it heaping with sweet potatoes and fruit, and received in exchange the coveted jackknife and pan. The next day we were to receive the king of Bouro on board and fire a salute in his honor. As we were all drawn up in uniform on the quarterdeck and his russet majesty appeared over the gangway in Malay regalia, who should he be but our friend of the day before, the proud possessor of the knife and pan! As long as those tubers lasted us, we reflected with pride on our close contact with royalty, and agreed that we had never tasted potatoes of a more regal flavor.

Another adventure brought with it a pretty moral. I was strolling alone on the beach one day,

Jesuit Convent in Macao; from The Expedition of an American Squadron

Courtesy University of Chicago Library

and presently noticed that I was followed by a tawny native. He had an ugly creese slung at his belt, which I took as an impressive sign that he might bear watching and therefore kept my weather eye on his movements. Just ahead, a magnificent tree overhung the beach, as large as a New England maple, its tropical verdure suffused with brilliant crimson, and the sands beneath gorgeously carpeted with the petals that had snowed down from the branches above. I stooped and picked up a blossom to examine it, when he of the creese ran up and tapped me on the shoulder, took the flower from my hand, went through the motions of smelling and eating it, and then represented the effect of the poison. I never saw more perfect acting. His cheeks blanched into a ghastly livid pallor, his eyes rolled up, and he seemed to be dying in the mere effort to simulate death. It was a lesson in charity that I never forgot. Instead of cutting me down with his creese, he opened his human heart and warned me of danger. We became brothers and friends on the spot.

Floating through the East Indian archipelago is like a dream of a fairy world. On every hand islands buried under a rank profusion of verdure, some of them mere islets like baskets of flowers drifting on the sea, some of them of continental size and piled with mountain ranges, like Java; occasionally a smoking volcano, whose distant glow by night gave us the friendly aid of a natural lighthouse; the air laden with fragrance from unknown plants and fruits hidden in the rank groves on shore–among them the peerless mangosteen, with a composite flavor of strawberry, orange, and heaven commingled; gentle breezes wafting us from one romantic scene to another, and slowly pushing us on through fairyland toward our ultimate goal in Cathay.* The *Saratoga* being a man-of-war and not a merchantman, there was no danger of our idyllic voyage being halted by a fleet of piratical proas popping round a headland and dashing upon us in quest of plunder and blood.

We took the Gilolo passage, or rather the passage took us, and crossing the line in longitude 129° east we swept out into the Pacific and made our way north under sunny skies by day and the full moon by night. Our first glimpse of savages, the pure unadulterated article, was interesting. We were passing two level islets some five degrees north of the line–voyagers in those distant seas would recognize them by their names on the chart, Pulo Anna and Pulo Mariere–when a score of canoes came prancing out over the waves laden with bananas and coconuts for barter. The men stood to their paddles and were tall, erect, splendid samples of stalwart manhood. Tailors were at a discount in their community; most of them wore only a loincloth, some of them indeed *decolleté* to their toes. Their light

*Cathay, an old name for China, was derived from "Khitai," and referred specifically to North China.–Ed.

olive-brown contrasted finely with the great green waves, and many of them heightened the effect still further by being embellished from head to foot with flamboyant tattooing. We bought and ate their coconuts, and presumed they would like to eat us. We should have disagreed with them, or at least tried to; and yet one could imagine a much worse fate than to be entombed in such handsome beasts.

All this time we were scuttling north in a clear sea. Our future clients, the Philippines, were to the west of our course—far out of sight. We made them a call the next year, enjoyed their tropical scenery, reveled in their fruit, made friends with the Tagallos, laid in Manila cheroots galore, and invested in peña dresses for girl friends at home; all the time without a suspicion of any deeper and more personal interest which the future might bring to us in those charming islands. But that was years before Aguinaldo was born, and Admiral Dewey was not yet even a sub-middy at Annapolis.*

In time we rounded the northern-end of Luzon, raced through the Balintang Straits before a stiff ten-knot breeze, passed the Balintang Islands, towering crags at whose base the Pacific was hammering with tremendous roar, and signalized our entrance into the China seas by taking a header into

*Emilio Aguinaldo (1869–1964), leader of Filipino independence forces first against the Spanish in 1896, then, in 1898, against the Americans. To his people he ranks as a Bolivar or a Washington. George Dewey, U.S.N. (1837–1917), the hero of the Battle of Manila Bay, May 1, 1898.—Ed.

the rear end of a typhoon. Luckily we did not hurt the typhoon nor the typhoon hurt us; but the experience could hardly be called playful. A day or two of ugly cross seas–cross in every sense–a ripping tempest, hatches battened down, life-lines led along the guns, decks swept fore and aft, the poor old wallowing ship punched, pounded, staggering, almost buried in the waves; everything wet, dirty, dismal; if anybody thinks it such a jolly lark, this going to sea, just come out to China and try a typhoon. But we pulled through, and so did the ship and the sun, which, blessed old public functionary, kindly dried us up and warmed our hearts. Three days after, we were wafted by gentle breezes in among the islands that fringe the southern coast of the Central Flowery Kingdom.*

As we were slowly working our way through the islands' serpentine channels, one of my messmates, a midshipman, sitting in the slings of the fore-topsail yard, beckoned me to come up and join him. We were neither of us handsome enough to pose as "the sweet little cherub that sits up aloft" nor angelic enough to "keep watch for the life of poor Jack"; but a hundred feet above the deck made a superb outlook, and we idled away a long cozy sunny afternoon taking a bird's-eye view of the outer rim of the Celestial Empire. All around us the waters were dotted with multitudinous fishing

*Both labels, the Central Flowery Kingdom and the Celestial Empire (see later), were applied to China.–Ed.

Macao from Penha Hill; from The Expedition of an American Squadron

Courtesy The Beverly R. Robinson Collection, United States Naval Academy Museum, Annapolis, Maryland

craft and sampans ambling their way to and fro. Farther off we could descry ranges of hills, picturesque forests, cultivated fields, busy villages, the whole landscape teeming with tokens of a populous empire; and over all one could imagine the shade of Confucius hovering with spectral benediction. Drifting quietly onward and threading the crooked passages that wind toward Macao,* we reached that quaint old Portuguese city at last and dropped anchor in the roadstead a couple of miles off the Praya. It was Tuesday, the eighth of April 1851; seven months and twenty thousand miles by log from home.

*Macao, a Portuguese trading outpost since 1557, on the estuary of the Pearl River sixty-five miles below Canton (Guangzhou).—Ed.

II

The Fate of the Donna Maria

IN THAT OPEN roadstead we lay rolling at our anchors sometimes for weeks at a time. Two years of waltzing to and fro and flitting up and down the coast, over to Manila, and up to the Madjicosima Islands intervened before the advent of Commodore Perry's Japan expedition, which, as events proved, the *Saratoga* would be kept to join. Whenever we returned to southern China from any of these sallies abroad, we divided our favors between Macao, Hong Kong,[1] Whampoa, Cum-sing-mun, and the Boca Tigris. Of all these ports, Macao is the most exposed. The winds have full sweep over a broad expanse and can raise at their own sweet will a choppy larruping sea. When you are lying at

[1]It was at Hong Kong–in one of our many visitations there–that we saw the Italian patriot, Garibaldi. He came beating up the harbor in command of a Peruvian barque, and as we heard his ringing voice and watched his masterful evolutions, we all agreed that if he was a great soldier he was an equally good sailor. He had escaped from Italy and was just then finding employment in South America, to return two years later to his native soil to take a hand in the next revolution. As he was to sail for San Francisco, we sent a letter bag home by him; and more than one of my correspondents had the pleasure of receiving letters that had been borne across the Pacific by the great champion of free Italy. It is not every day you can have a Garibaldi for your mail carrier!

anchor off Macao, therefore, you are very literally "rocked in the cradle of the deep."

Our first experience in that thumping bumping cradle was delicious. We of the steerage–middies, past midshipmen, and clerk–slept in hammocks; and as we swayed with the swing of the ship, we were not only rocked to sleep but oftentimes sung to sleep by a submarine serenade–a sort of music in solution. The performers were myriads of little fishes, and sweeter lullaby no man could wish. Macao was the only port where we enjoyed these liquid concerts, though very likely musical fishes may frequent other points on the Chinese coast. Travelers have heard them off the rivers of Cambodia to the south, along the shores of Ceylon, and along various parts of the African coast. Charles Kingsley* heard them in the West Indies. Others have noted them along our southern Atlantic coast, in the Gulf of Mexico, and up and down the shores of the Pacific. There appear to be many varieties and different grades of subaqueous musicians–from the grunting gurnard and purring seahorse to the deep-sea drumfish and the "mysterious music of the Pascagoula." Why should there not be diverse tones in a fish orchestra as in a human orchestra? Why should not the troubadours of the deep have their horns, oboes, flutes, harps, kettledrums, triangles, and all the rest of the orchestral choir,

*Charles Kingsley (1819–75), English author and clergyman, an advocate of Christian Socialism.–Ed.

View of Hong Kong from East Point; from The Expedition of an American Squadron

Courtesy University of Chicago Library

like their brothers of the wind and string on land?

The weird sounds Kingsley heard as he listened from the veranda of a friend's house on the isle of Monos were like this: "Between the howls of the wind I became aware of a strange noise from seaward–a booming, or rather humming, most like that which a locomotive sometimes makes when blowing off steam. It was faint and distant, but deep and strong enough to set one guessing its cause." He hears the same sound the next morning in a dead calm, and learns from the natives "that it came from under the water and was most probably made by none other than the famous musical or drum-fish, of whom one had heard and hardly believed much in past years." He quotes the description given by another observer who, while on board a schooner at anchor off Chaguaramas, heard a variety of notes. "Immediately under the vessel I heard a deep and not unpleasant sound, similar to those one might imagine to proceed from a thousand Æolian harps; this ceased, and deep twanging notes succeeded; these gradually swelled into an uninterrupted stream of singular sounds like the booming of a number of Chinese gongs under the water; to these succeeded notes that had a faint resemblance to a wild chorus of a hundred human voices singing out of tune in deep bass."

Kingsley refers to still another listener on the Pacific coast and up the rivers of Ecuador who heard the music from the water and at first thought the sound "was produced by a fly or hornet of extraordinary size; but afterward, having advanced a little farther, he heard a multitude of different voices which harmonized together, imitating a church organ to great perfection."[2] A naval officer who heard this submarine music at the mouth of a river in Cambodia says it sounded like "a mixture of the bass of an organ, the ringing of bells, the guttural cries of a large frog, and the tones of an enormous harp."[3] Other comparisons have been used. A visitor in Mississippi was called down to the river one day by an old fisherman "to hear the spirits singing under the water." It was "the mysterious music of the Pascagoula." Out of the depths of that river "rose a roaring, murmuring sound which gradually increased in strength and in volume, then diminished"; "a strange and tremulous sound," like the humming of telegraph wires; and "a roaring, rushing sound." The writer even illustrates the notes by using a musical scale; sometimes there were different tones in the harmony, and rising from the keynote to an octave above; sometimes quick sharp sounds in single notes or in pairs; and at any sudden noise, like the splashing of an oar, the music would instantly cease.

Another observer says, "a low plaintive sound is heard rising and falling like that of an Æolian

[2]Charles Kingsley. *At Last; a Christmas in the West Indies.* pp. 157–61.

[3]*Popular Science Monthly,* xxiii; p. 571.

harp"; "the sounds are sweet and plaintive, but monotonous."[4] And still another, cruising in his yacht along the shores of Florida a dozen years ago, writes that while at anchor in Old Tampa Bay he heard "a single note, continuous for a long time. It recalled the singing of telegraph wires, or the hum of a planing mill, or the music of an Æolian harp." It had no resemblance to the drumfish, which he says is common in Florida and whose note is "a booming, interrupted noise."[5]

It is quite a surprise to the lay mind—and that is the sort I carry—to find how many fishes are known to science as endowed with vocal powers. While engaged in hunting up and making the acquaintance of some of these scaly sirens on my own independent hook, a literary friend has called my attention to a number of scientific authorities who count up more than fifty kinds. I could give the reader a list of them—or at least of the fishy prima donnas—all in their Latin dress, which would be immensely learned and edifying; but it might take me beyond my depth, as the fish are already, so I will be discreet and refrain.

It was surely not the drumfish, nor the barking dogfish, nor the grunting gurnard that serenaded us in Macao roads on those still, tropical, starlighted nights. Our music came from another section of the finny orchestra—perhaps from the string quartet

[4] *Popular Science Monthly,* xxxvi; pp. 791–94.
[5] *Popular Science Monthly,* xxxvii; p. 410.

rather than the brass band and kettledrums. It was a gentle tinkling or gurgling as of the breaking of silvery bubbles all over the bottom of the ship, or like the ringing of myriads of little bells down under the deep. I am inclined to think the music was produced by schools of mullet; if so, they would have been even more welcome in the frying pan than at the harpsichord. The tones floated around us by the hour together—sometimes swelling into a deep and solemn strain, sometimes faintly pattering like the feet of fairies dancing. Had I been born a poet I should have set the music to rhyme. But being only one of Uncle Sam's youngsters, a prosy clerk, it lulled me to sleep and perhaps rippled through my dreams with echoes of home.

One can understand a chorus of frogs in a swamp or the matins and vespers of birds in forest and field. But what was this? Have the tribes of the wave a language that they use as we do ours? Or is it merely an instinct, an impulse to put into action some curious power they find they possess?—and so in their exuberance every little fish goes to pounding, pattering, tinkling, murmuring, dancing with all his might at his own sweet will and without reference to his myriad brother minnows in the same shoal. Perhaps it may be the call of love. Since Venus was born on the wave, she may have left the briny deep all tinctured with an infusion of love and all the finny tribes touched with the spell. May not even fish have their pretty ways of attracting the admiration of their scaly paramours? And if so, what could be prettier and sweeter than this? This is what Darwin makes it. Yet sometimes it is such a mournful monotone that one thinks of a dirge instead; whole circles of family friends may have been scooped in the dragnet and fallen a prey to the voracity of that monster, man—and the tearful survivors may be celebrating a submarine mass for the repose of the victims in the monster's stomach. Or if those mermaids have a religion, this liquid music may be the worship they offer to Neptune; or possibly their vain endeavor to placate and win their archenemy, man.

So much for our first experience in the Central Flowery Kingdom. Our second was of quite another sort.

The sloop-of-war *St. Mary's*, which we had come to China to relieve, had sailed on her return voyage without waiting for us, and Captain Walker found himself the senior officer on the station. Finding it agreeable on shore and having no commodore to order him off to sea, he accepted an invitation to exist for a while on the cool verandas of Consul De Silva and sent off orders to get the ship round into the Typa. This is a placid expanse separated from the main roadstead by Typa Island and well protected by other islands from the unmannerly winds that, at times, make the outer harbor so rough. It took several tides and an immense amount of kedge-hauling, boatswain whistling, and capstan work to warp the *Saratoga* in over the two shallow bars; but the bars were soft mud, and she dragged through without harm. When at last she shook herself free, with all sail set and driven by a lively breeze and the stentorian voice of our first lieutenant, she flew to her berth and executed a pretty "flying moor"—a beautiful evolution that was a fancy trick with the old-timers but in these degenerate days of steam has, I presume, fallen into "innocuous desuetude."

This transfer to the Typa was not a matter of thrilling interest in itself, but it did put us in contact with a startling bit of history that deserves recording. It is to be found now I imagine only in the naval archives at Lisbon, perhaps long ago forgotten even there.

Our berth was between the U.S.S. *Marion* on the the one side and, on the other, the remains of a Portuguese frigate, the *Donna Maria*, whose blackened timbers bore silent witness to her melancholy fate. It was only five months before—October 29, 1850—that she met her doom. It was the birthday of the queen of Portugal. In honor of the day, both ships were dressed from stem to stern in the flags of all nations and presented a brilliant picture of emblazonry. At noon the frigate fired a royal salute, which was answered by the *Marion* and by the forts on shore. On board the *Marion* the guns were secured, the crew were piped to dinner, the messes were cleared, and the long sultry afternoon began to wear placidly away. The men were gathered in little groups between the guns—sewing, reading, spinning yarns, or sleeping in the shade. The clean white decks, the awnings spread, the boats at the booms with a boatkeeper in each, the officer of the deck quietly pacing his watch, most of the other officers taking their siesta below. Such familiar details will serve to complete the picture of routine man-of-war life in the tropics. In the midst of this tranquil scene and without a moment's warning, a terrific explosion brought every man to his feet. Wakened by the shock and supposing the *Marion* had for some unaccountable reason received a broadside from the frigate, the lieutenant rushed on deck in his pajamas shouting "Clear away the batteries!" But instead, the frigate herself had blown up, and as the smoke drifted away the real horror was recognized.

All that saved the *Marion* was the fact that she lay so near. Almost everything went over her. Two big guns went roaring between her masts with a volcanic shower of bolts, deadeyes, broken spars, and fragments of human bodies. One of the guns fell within a few feet of her and threw back on board a furious splash of spray. The whole atmosphere was thick with torn missiles, tangled debris of planks, rigging, blocks, spars, sails, handspikes, battle-axes, and all the diversified paraphernalia that enter into the makeup of a man-of-war. Over a circuit of a mile in diameter around the smoking frigate, the calm waters were churned into roar and foam by the descending shower. The boats were instantly called away and dashed to the scene in order to extricate from the tangle of cordage and burning timbers any victims in whom there might still be left a sign of life. The work of rescue soon lapsed into the more solemn task of gathering the dead. Out of the entire crew of 250 only five remained–one Portuguese, two Chinamen, and two Lascars.* Yet a second explosion, of a small deck magazine, drove the boats from their labor. After it was seen that no life remained, the burning ship was left to her fate. As the soundings were but little over three fathoms, she could not sink beneath the surface. Resting on the bottom, in the course of the night, she burned to the water's edge.

The *Marion* suffered no damage beyond a broken arm or two and a few bruises, a boat stove at the booms, the awnings slashed, and both awnings and snowy deck bespattered with blood. Her men were often sobered by the gruesome sight of bodies that for days after went floating past, until gathered up and buried by the Portuguese patrol boats. One day the sentry at the gangway was horrified at the sudden rising of a Portuguese sentry from the deep alongside, with musket still grimly held at "carry arms" as in life.

The fate of the *Donna Maria* will probably remain a mystery to the end of time. No man knows

*Lascar, British designation for an East Indian seaman.–Ed.

whence came the spark that fired her magazine. The magazine had been opened that noon, of course, to get the ammunition for the salute. But the explosion did not come until two or three hours later; and such an interval, together with the stringent regulations that control the handling of explosives on a man-of-war, would seem to preclude the theory of an accident. The commander of the frigate was commonly reputed to be a man of despotic and passionate temper; and the story was current in Macao that for some cause, real or fancied, he flew into a rage with the gunner, sent for him to his cabin, cursed him, pulled his beard, and even assaulted him with kicks and blows. The gunner replied that he had been many years in the service and had never been subjected to such indignities before; that he was an old man and had not long to live, but that when he did die many more should go to hell with him; with which threat he left the captain's presence. Brooding over the treatment he had received and, as many believed, becoming crazed with anger, he may have taken the opportunity of the salute to leave a lighted fuse in the magazine, which, in time, reached the powder and sent the ship to her doom. But he went with the rest—and no man knows.

III

After Mutineers in Patchungsan

OUR BUSINESS in China was to protect the interests of American citizens and American commerce in the East. The Taiping Rebellion* had already started in the southern provinces, and our first active duty was to visit Whampoa and put our merchants in Canton under the protection of American guns. Later the same year we strolled over to Manila and spent a lazy month amid its torrid luxuries. But neither of these is the subject of my story. Manila has written her own record since, and the Taipings will keep; we can return to them later. Just now we will look in on a group of emerald isles some three hundred miles off the Celestial coast.

In the spring of 1852, an American ship, the *Robert Browne*, sailed from Amoy with a cargo of coolies for San Francisco. Some weeks out, the coolies rose upon the crew, murdering all but five. They

*China's Taiping Rebellion (1850–64), which nearly overturned the Ch'ing (Manchu) Dynasty, burst out of Christian sectarianism, while it also was a classic peasant uprising. Taiping's prophet was Hung Hsui-ch'uan, who passionately preached a gospel of Old Testament-based Protestant Christianity with a brotherhood of revolutionary nationalism and egalitarianism. See Chapter VIII.–Ed.

compelled the survivors to navigate the ship back to China. By the time they sighted the Madjicosimas on their return, they had become panic-stricken at the possible consequences of their crime, and concluded to take refuge on the islands. The sailors made for Patchungsan accordingly and, grounding the ship on a reef near the shore, manned the long-boat and began ferrying the mutineers to the beach. Some three hundred of them were thus landed, and the boat came back for the last twenty-five. Instead of taking them ashore, however, the Yankee tars dashed up over the gangway and seizing the nearest handspikes and belaying pins overpowered the coolies and lashed them to ringbolts in the deck. Then they ran to the braces, rounded in the fore and main yards, backed the ship off the reef, and squared away for the open sea, leaving the crowds of baffled mutineers like a pack of savages yelling, cursing, tearing up and down the beach in impotent rage. It was some three hundred or four hundred miles to Amoy, and thither with their perilous freight they directed their course. Never daring to sleep, scarcely snatching a moment to eat, they kept their vigils by night and by day, at the wheel, on the lookout, at the braces, watching the sails and the weather, standing sentry over their prisoners. Many times did the miscreants gnaw their fastenings and threaten another tragedy like the first, but were as often refettered. Fortunately no storm darkened the sky. Fortunately too, as they approached the

Pagoda and Anchorage at Whampoa (Huang-pu); from The Expedition of an American Squadron

Courtesy The Beverly R. Robinson Collection, United States Naval Academy Museum, Annapolis, Maryland

coast, half a dozen mates of merchantmen lying at anchor in Amoy were out on a rollicking cruise down the harbor when the *Robert Browne* hove in sight. She was behaving strangely and her flag was union down. Plainly something was the matter, and these tough-fisted pleasure-seekers dashed out over the waves to see. Not a moment too soon; for as they mounted over the rail, the prisoners had just torn themselves free and were in the act of charging upon their exhausted captors, who in a few seconds more would have been food for sharks. Like a thunderbolt the rescuers were upon them, and once more the baffled coolies were firmly secured to the ship's deck.

When we reached Amoy the *Robert Browne* was lying quietly at anchor, and the prisoners were turned over to us. Two days later an English man-of-war, the brig *Lily*, returned from the islands with another score, and these also were added to our charge. She had found the mutineers in a woeful plight, sick, desperate, half-starved. The natives, a gentle inoffensive people, had helped them put up bamboo barracks near the shore, and there they were living on whatever the islanders, not overfed themselves, could bring them. When the *Lily* appeared round the point, they recognized her as a messenger of doom and scuttled incontinently for the forest-clad mountains in the interior; so terrified that, as the interpreter declared, no less than forty of those who could not keep up with their fleeing comrades, took their own lives or fell and died from sheer exhaustion.

It was to gather in another batch of these poor wretches that the *Saratoga* was ordered on a cruise to the Madjicosimas. Three days' sail from Amoy, rounding the northern end of Formosa and wafted over smooth seas by kindly breezes, we found ourselves in a beautiful cluster of islands, of which Patchungsan, named from its "eight huge hills," was not only the chief but the fairest. That was our destination.

A charming picture it made as we approached; mountains draped with tropical verdure, in which one could distinguish the breadfruit, the acacia, the broad fronds of the palm, and even the familiar Norway pine; and sloping down from the hills to the shore were green fields, separated sometimes by deep glades and watercourses, sometimes by craggy fences of coral. We wondered whether such lovely scenery could be conscious of holding in its placid bosom a nest of bloody bandits. We rounded to in the spacious harbor, dropped anchor, furled sails, and sent a boat on shore.

There stood the bamboo barracks, just as they had been described to us. We watched the party of natives who met our interpreter on the beach and took him up to one of the huts for a palaver. It proved to be as on the arrival of H. M. brig *Lily*. The birds had flown. The apparition of another avenging fury in the shape of another man-of-war

View of Old China Street in Canton; from The Expedition of an American Squadron

Courtesy University of Chicago Library

lent wings to their terror, and all but the sick and dying had bolted again for the woods in the wildest helter-skelter of alarm. When the boat returned with such information as was obtainable, the captain decided to send out an expedition or two in pursuit. Every man on board was eager to volunteer. It would be such a lark; it was just going ashore on liberty, in a wild tropical island, and with a spice of adventure thrown in. Some four or five score of the men were selected for the privilege.

The next morning the sun rose in a cloudless sky. The island with its beauties of mountain, valley, forest, and lawn lay peacefully spread before us with scarcely a breath of air to ruffle the verdure of its fragrant thickets; and circling around it the liquid sea, as innocent and bland as if it had never been conscious of such a thing as a storm. On such a placid day one almost listened for the home church bells, for it was Sunday. But no Sunday for us, and no church bells; instead, a hustling day of martial order and disorder. On shore, hid in the caverns, lurking in the bush, housed in the huts, were the fugitive mutineers; on board the ship the din, bustle, and turmoil of preparations to catch them. The organization of a night campaign, the necessary equipment and drill, together with the complex labors of the commissariat, turned our gentle Sunday into chaos. Officers were assigned and four divisions told off, numbering each some score of doughty warriors. On deck the leaders were mustering their men; sergeants and corporals were putting awkward squads through the manual; quarter-gunners were distributing muskets, pistols, and cutlasses; the sailmaker's gang were stitching haversacks of canvas; and mess cooks below were concocting the rations to fill them; while glowering aloof in sullen disappointment rejected volunteers strolled to and fro, gazing idly over the bulwarks, affecting indifference, and consigning to the everlasting shade the whole blooming enterprise.

By nine o'clock at night the armament began embarking; by eleven the last man was ashore. There the guides met them and the four parties began their long and devious tramp in the dark. The outlaws had fled up the valleys, over the hills, through the woods, among the rocks, caves, mountain passes, wherever fear drove them or hope held out the promise of shelter. But up the valleys, over the hills, through the woods, among the rocks, caves, and mountain passes, like the avenging spirit of Cain, their pursuers steadily followed on their track. As I did not have the pleasure of accompanying this "personally conducted" tour but did go on the second expedition, I will not undertake to penetrate the darkness of that night and imagine adventures I did not share. The party returned the next day bringing some fifty more of the fugitives, who were duly added to our list.

Meanwhile, all the prisoners were taken on shore and snugly quartered in the bamboo barracks, with relays of sentries from our marine guard pacing their beat around them. It looked really quite martial. Tuesday morning opened bright, with a spanking fresh breeze and a lively sea, but neither of them rampant enough to interrupt the flying boats that were conveying orders and provender to the party on shore. In the last boat that pushed off from the gangway that morning, a couple of youngsters from the port steerage mess started for a morning stroll. After so many salt-water duckings, we cherished ambitions for a fresh water bath if the island could boast a stream big enough; and anyhow a frolic on the greensward would limber up our sea legs. We got what we were after–and a lot more. That boat was the last to reach the shore for two mortal days. We were safely on *terra firma*, and there we had to stay through a villainous typhoon.

The barometer was somewhat demoralized when we left the ship. But that was in the cabin; and as we had no barometer in the steerage–only took such weather as was dealt out to us–we had started on our tramp in blissful ignorance. First of all a look at our prisoners in the bamboo barracks. Poor knaves–there they were, nearly a hundred of them, old and young, sick and well, huddled together on the earth floor of the building, whose roof of thatch shielded them from the torrid sun, while the open sides admitted the cool breeze. The more defiant were in double irons, the weaker only manacled; the sick and the boys were at large. Some appeared dazed by the calamity that had overtaken them, and lay prostrate on their straw mats heedless of what was passing around.

A few ugly-visaged ruffians, afterwards identified as among the ringleaders of the mutiny, sat bolt upright among their companions, reckless of the crime and scornfully indifferent to its retribution. One little chap some ten years old was lying on the ground covered with a tattered mat, the last ray of hope fled from his boyish face, the dripping tears telling more plainly than words what despair had settled on his young heart. When we carried him to his home in Amoy a month or two after, kind treatment had transformed him into another child, and we could hardly persuade him then to leave his new friends.

The freshening breeze piped and whistled over the grassy hills as we left the camp for a stroll. It was an interesting country. We peeped into the cave on the point, much to the displeasure of its tenants the bats, made morning calls on the simple natives in their neatly thatched huts, climbed a crag for the view, strayed into a deserted temple whose Dagon had fallen from the crumbling altar and whose devotees brought no more oblations of smoking incense; and all the while exploring the landscape for that freshwater brook in which we were to take that freshwater bath. No brook appeared; but we got the bath all the same, of very fresh water, and in overwhelming abundance.

Back to the shore, hoping for a boat from the ship. No boat. No chance for a boat. Wind increasing. Horizon murky and lurid. A dirty scud beginning to drive through the sky. The sun tried for a time to burn through in spots, and finding itself shut out of its own firmament by nasty clouds finally withdrew in dudgeon to parts unknown. The gale was rising, and before long a sharp drizzle was sweeping through the air on the yelling blasts that penetrated our dapper white costume and cut like showers of needles. We were glad enough to flee for shelter to the big cabin where the guard was quartered. In the course of the afternoon we attempted to build a rookery of our own.

The tempest laughed itself hoarse at our efforts. Nothing we could put up was any protection against the pitiless rain. And presently, an ill-mannered blast ripped up the whole fabric and blew its fragments out of sight. It was by a logical necessity therefore–hurricane logic, not easy to answer–that we spent that roaring night in the big cabin with the guard. Wet, tired, and sore, we tried to bury ourselves in a scant pile of straw down in the corner and shiver ourselves to sleep. It was a kind of cold storage, and the drowsy goddess had no notion of being wooed in that fashion. The weary night dragged slowly on, and would have been more interminable still but for a sudden alarm that the hungry pirates were coming down on the camp for a foraging attack. All hands hustled out to meet them. We congratulated ourselves that the exercise would at least keep us warm. The attack did not materialize. All the comfort we got out of it was that the officer of the guard gave us each a cutlass, and the belt, tightly buckled around our equatorial regions, made life a trifle less wintry.

The only other episode of that miserable night was the sudden outcry of a rough old salt, "Corporal of the guard! There's a son-of-a-gun a hangin' himself!" One of the prisoners, tired of his misery and uncertain as to what further retribution might be in store for him, decided to take himself out of the case and, with the long folds of his turban thrown over a bamboo rafter, made a vigorous push for the unseen. He was easily cut down and persuaded to resume his earthly pilgrimage for a while longer.

At daybreak we struggled outside, at the risk of being blown into the next lot. Whoop! How that hurricane scoured over the sea and land, yelling, screeching, foaming at the mouth, cutting off the tops of the waves and hurling them through the air. It was magnificent, but tragic and grim. The poor ship had spent as uncomfortable a night as we. There she lay wallowing, all her top hamper down on deck, three anchors out ahead, now rising wearily over the enormous billows and then plunging headlong to bury herself in a smother of spray, tugging at her chains like a Titan, as if determined to tear them away and rush to her doom on the reef.

The big waves came piling in from the sea in indescribable masses, raging, furious, passionate, literally tumbling over each other in the mad rush to get at her, plunging on the ship like demons, trying to overwhelm her and send her to the bottom, or roaring past to break on the reef in towering hills of foam. That reef was the loop that united the island with its nearest neighbor, Kokiensan; there was nothing beyond but the wild Pacific, and no passage through. If those cables should give way, five minutes would seal her doom and that of every living thing on board. On that frightful coral bridge, the pounding of those surges would smash her to atoms. Such a fate for our shipmates set our hearts to thumping.

We watched the conflict for hours with breathless interest; and all the more dismally because such a catastrophe would leave us, a handful of white men, on an island far out of the track of passing ships, and with those three hundred mutineers in the mountains in our rear, disappointed, hungry, savage, and desperate. It was a funereal day that, *Like a wounded snake dragged its slow length along.*

But at last it came to an end. Things generally do. The most furious blasts began to tame down. The murky heavens began to lose something of their sullen blackness. The rain squalls came thinner and weaker. The typhoon began to show signs of exhaustion as if it had about blown itself out. By nightfall of the second day, nature was tired of chaos and wanted to rest. The kindly natives brought us riceballs to keep us from starving, and then helped us rebuild our demolished hut. Into the straw we bundled and knew nothing more until at daybreak a middy shouted in our ears, "Tumble out there, sleepers! Boat coming ashore!" Getting back on board was like getting home. The first lieutenant had the deck, and all hands were at the capstan bars heaving up the extra anchors. All hands had a chance to witness the prodigals' return. As we mounted over the gangway and waddled aft to report ourselves to the smiling officer, our spandy white toggery turned to a bedraggled butternut gray, all hands smiled with him, some of them audibly. But we dove below and soon got back into civilization and clean clothes.

The second expedition was another midnight prowl like the first. I hastened to volunteer, but with an ardor that would hardly pass for patriotic or even martial. The island was said to abound in pigeons; and having risen to the dignity of caterer to the port steerage mess, my quest was not pirates but game. It was not unreasonable to expect that while the rest of the cohort were scooping up the mutineers, a few pigeons would obligingly put themselves under my care. To that end, I borrowed a fowling-piece and joined the expedition in the role of the mighty hunter.

We landed in the dark Friday night, a compact force of eight officers and seventy or eighty bluejackets well armed. Our guides met us at the beach. So did a shower. We had scarcely set foot on *terra firma* before the rain came to welcome us–to cheer but not inebriate; at first a gentle drizzle, then a firm crescendo, and at last a tropical deluge. We began our march by nine o'clock and tramped for hours under a kind of cloudburst; the night black as pitch; every gully a roaring torrent; every coral fence ragged and multitudinous in scratches and tumbles; the cactus hedges disobligingly skillful in rending our garments and gashing our shins. At first our path for a long distance skirted the shore. Then, as the curving line of the bay diverged from the path, we struck boldly into the interior, leaving on our right a dense grove of pines, and rising on the uplands by a deep-worn rut tangled with interlacing roots and plashing with mire. Till midnight we pushed on through the heavy rain, and the rain through us. And by the time we straggled in at the appointed rendezvous site, a deserted temple in a grove, we looked more like a set of shipwrecked pirates ourselves than a company of honest men in pursuit of those gentry. All our military ardor was soaked out of us, and a large proportion of our morals. Both were somewhat replenished by a hasty lunch. The silent old temple took charge of our haversacks and other freight; and thus relieved we separated, and the four divisions radiated out into the darkness like the sticks of a fan. Each corps vivisected itself into several scouting parties, so that in the course of the night we covered and explored a wide territory. It was a still hunt for native cabins. When one was found we silently surrounded it so that nothing could escape and then, suddenly opening the door and thrusting in a lighted torch, we ransacked the hut for hidden pirates. It was not polite, and the gentle inmates were badly frightened; but we did them no harm and had our labor for our pains.

In due time the night wore away and with returning dawn our corps tramped back to the rendezvous. Pirate-hunting does very well for a side issue, but my business being pigeons, I took my bearings from the sacred grove and started out on a foraging tour of my own. I hunted for pigeons as faithfully as we had hunted for pirates—and with the same result. Pastures, woods, rocks, hills—I scoured them all. Not a bird. Not a ghost of a bird. Pigeons and pirates had evidently made common cause and had flown to the mountains together. The best part of the hunt was getting back to a hot breakfast at the old temple. And after all, looking at it philosophically, what right had I, a foreign interloper, to kill and eat Madjicosima pigeons, anymore than they had to kill and eat me? We had a claim on the pirates but what claim on the pigeons? So with the first squad that started, my gun and I slowly wended our way back to the ship sadder and wiser, also considerably wetter. By mid-afternoon all the divisions were safely back, and the two or three prisoners they had taken were added to the choice lot already on board. At daybreak, it was up anchor and off for Hong Kong.

What became of the mutineers? Deponent saith not; but I will give you the facts and you can judge for yourself. Upon our return to Hong Kong, the cabin of the *Saratoga* was turned into a courtroom; the prisoners were brought in one by one and confronted with the survivors of the ill-fated *Robert Browne.* The ringleaders were identified and in due time were forwarded to Canton and turned over to the Chinese courts. Perhaps they paid the penalty of their crime. Perhaps their judges, not overfond of foreign barbarians, winked at it as on the whole a meritorious act. We never knew. But the rest of the rout we ourselves carried back to Amoy and quietly dismissed to their homes.

IV

Cruising for Pirates and What We Caught

THE FOLLOWING September, the *Saratoga* was again dispatched on a mission of vengeance. A Boston merchantman, the *Celestial*, while peaceably wending her way to Hong Kong, had run the gauntlet of a whole fleet of Chinese freebooters but had managed to elude them and escape. We were sent out to catch the miscreants, or any other red-rovers we might find practicing their art, and teach them the error of their ways.

Our orders were to cruise for a month down the coast as far as the Gulf of Tonquin–the first week off the Ladrones, the remaining three off the Taya Islands and Hainan. It was ugly weather, squally and threatening when we got up anchor and disappeared from Hong Kong. But it took us out clear of the islands in dashing style, and three or four hours brought us to our cruising ground. There under easy sail we stood off all day and night to the southward and westward, sharply scanning every sort of craft we met and looking into the harbors for any bandits that might be lurking there. The next forenoon we wore round and made a long stretch back toward the Ladrones. We gave chase to a sinister-looking scow that proved to be an innocent trader bound to Macao, whither he had fled, badly frightened as soon as we let him off. One evening we met a fleet of eight junks coming in, and we promptly put about and overhauled them. They were as panic-stricken as the other. The sudden apparition of a big man-of-war pouncing upon them like a hawk upon a brood of chickens sent them scampering off to all points of the compass, burning joss paper and wildly beating their gongs for help from the Chinese pantheon.

At last the week off the Ladrones was duly completed. The helm was put up and round we went, bound for "fresh fields and pastures new." A fair breeze was sweeping us smoothly down the seas when suddenly our foreyard* determined otherwise. To the best of our knowledge and belief it had always been robust and healthy, a well-behaved stick of sound and positive convictions. But all at once it was discovered that an internal disorder was preying on its vitals; whereupon the carpenter bluntly reported to the officer of the deck, and the officer of the deck to the first lieutenant, and the first lieutenant to the captain, that the foreyard was rotten in the slings. No sailor need be reminded what that would mean in a gale of wind. Round the ship spun again on her heel and bracing sharp up began to beat back for the nearest known port;

*A foreyard was the lowest yard (a stout, rounded, long spar) on a sailing ship's foremast; a yard's function was to support and spread the head of a square sail.–Ed.

Returning to Hong Kong with Three Pirate Vessels;
from The Wild Coasts of Nipon [*sic*]

Courtesy University of Chicago Library

which haven of refuge proved to be a cove in an island variously called Sancian, Sanchuen, and St. John's. Occupied by fishermen, it was a quiet place some seventy-five miles to the southwest of Macao. High bluffs, projecting ledges, with patches of sandy beach below and between, and the whole plentifully bestrewn with boulders, which were the relics of some far away glacial period–that was the type of scenery.

At the head of a bay some three or four miles off, we could see a fishing hamlet and a fleet of small craft at anchor before it or slipping in and out with the tide. Close by us, a few rocky farms, out of which the tenants managed to scratch a living by coaxing out of the gravel small crops of bananas, oranges, pineapples, sweet potatoes, and beans, wherever the jealous boulders would permit.

This was the place where the Portuguese were first permitted to trade in 1517, before the founding of Macao. For a few years they had here a bustling colony. But a neighbor island, Lampacao, proved more attractive and gradually drew away from Sancian both the trade and the traders. Macao in turn did the same for Lampacao, and the site was so entirely abandoned that now the very location of the ancient city is quite unknown.

The dim memory of Lampacao and all her vanished commerce was as nothing, however, beside our interest in one man, who finished a great life and breathed his last on the shores of this obscure islet. It was in 1552 that St. Francis Xavier* died on Sancian. It was in 1852, just three centuries after, that a party of us stood reverently on the strand from which the body of the heroic missionary had been borne away to be entombed in a distant church in Goa. From that day to this, though of different faith, I have felt a sense of possession in the memory and deeds of the famous East Indian apostle, simply from having walked the beach he trod and looked on the rugged scenery that was the last vision to his closing eyes.

The delinquent spar was speedily down on deck, stripped of its harness, laid on its back, and made ready for surgery. A bad case of appendicitis, or internal cancer, or worse. The carpenter and his crew went at it *con amore*, dug out the cankerous sludge, filled in with sound timber, and fished the whole with extra spars laid on and heavily clamped along the middle of the yard. A reasonably fair job, and as strong as tools and wood could make it, but awkward and bungling; the carpenter himself declared that he would not trust it in a gale of wind. If we had had that stick aloft in the typhoon we encountered a fortnight later, very likely we should have lost our masts and gone to the bottom; in which case any possible readers who may be sauntering

*St. Francis Xavier (1506–52), Basque Jesuit missionary, venerated as the Apostle to the Indies. Although he died in China, he is buried in Goa, in western India, located on the Arabian Sea, where he started numerous missions.—Ed.

with me through these devious pages would have been spared the labor. But the carpenter's verdict and an official survey of the bandaged spar changed all that. The captain decided to put back to Macao and get a new foreyard.

I need not hint to you how incensed the commodore was that we should dare to leave our cruising ground, nor how he set all the carpenters to work from all three ships to make the new spar out of our spare main topmast and the *Susquehanna's* spare jib-boom, and when done, hustled us out of port in short order to finish our cruise. At any rate, we got out of that neighborhood as fast as canvas and breeze could take us and went to look for the other pirates. Outside, a fair wind swept us down off the Taya Islands. There we tried a ruse; ran the guns in, closed the ports, concealed our multitudinous crew, and did our best to look like an innocent merchantman, hoping to decoy some red-rover, or perhaps a whole fleet of them, to an attack. No result; pious fraud does not seem to work with pirates. So we kept on down the coast, passed the false Tinhosa, and ran in for Tinhosa the real, which proved to be a steep, rocky, mountainous island nearly halfway down the eastern shore of Hainan. Another long stretch, and the delusive current swept us far to the southward and westward of Gaalong Bay, and doubtless chuckled all over its foamy surface to see us laboriously beating back in the teeth of an increasing gale. If you have ever gone fishing for pirates in these outlandish parts, these unfamiliar names may assist the geographical side of your memory. We meant to run to Gaalong Bay for shelter, but in the rising storm we could not fetch in, and so ran for the open main in order to get plenty of sea room in which to meet whatever was coming.

And it was coming, sure. This "Thing" of the sea had been getting itself together and lying in wait for us; a demoniac octopus of the air whose tentacles were already spitefully snatching at us from afar. Let us get a look at the monster before it actually arrives, as we did not at the Madjicosima storm a few pages back.

Our unlucky cruise was just about timed with the autumnal change of monsoon. In the China seas the regular semi-annual shift of atmospheric currents occurs in September and October; when, the sun having returned into the southern hemisphere, the southwest monsoon gradually retreats from its invasion of northern zones and the northeast trades chase it back to its home. It is not a sudden change. There is a kind of tricky recess, a belt of calms and erratic weather. This is the happy hunting ground of the typhoon. As M. Reclus explains in his entertaining book, *The Ocean*, "It is at this epoch of the change of the seasons that the powerful aerial masses, charged with electricity, engage in strife for the supremacy, and by their encounter produce those great eddies which are developed in spirals across the seas and the continents." The statement which he draws from another meteorologist that of 365 West Indian hurricanes recorded between 1493 and 1855, more than two-thirds came in October, when "the strongly heated coasts of South America begin to attract toward themselves the colder and denser air of the northern continent," might stand as a fair account of the situation in the East Indies also. The furnace heat of the tropics, the enormous expansion and elevation of the lower atmospheric levels, the velocity of the other masses rushing in, their collision with island peaks and mountain ranges, their sharp concussion with each other and the attendant electric explosions—these are the fierce dynamics of the air out of which are gendered those revolving storms that descend to the earth and go spinning their dance of death over a much enduring surface.

In point of size, they vary from the tornado, which mows its narrow swath through the woods, to the full-grown cyclone whose circle sweeps half an ocean. The hurricane of 1839 was about three hundred miles in diameter at the Antilles, five hundred when it reached the Bermudas, and nearly eighteen hundred when it crashed upon Ireland. A furious cyclone encountered between Japan and Formosa in July 1853 by the *Saratoga* and three other vessels of the Japan expedition, which was afterwards described and mapped by Mr. Redfield, was at least a thousand miles in diameter. Still larger was the storm that overtook our flagship the *Mississippi*, not far from the same region in October of the following year. It was from fifteen hundred to two thousand miles across, and traveled for six days at a rate of from twelve to forty miles an hour. By contrast, the tornado that crossed the state of Indiana in April 1852, leaving a track littered with wreckage of forests and cattle and towns, was only a mile wide. The destructive cyclone in Iowa in 1882 averaged half a mile. One which obliterated a village near Springfield, Missouri, in April 1880, sweeping its very site so bare that scarcely the splinters could be found, cut a path nowhere broader than 150 rods.* And, finally, the tornado that tore its way through Tuscumbia, Alabama, on a quiet Sabbath evening in the autumn of 1874, bursting the stoutest buildings into fragments and killing a number of the inhabitants, measured in diameter less than four hundred feet.

The height of the column is as variable as its diameter. Two miles is an unusual elevation; and the other extreme might be not more than a hundred yards. A lofty mountain range is a wall against which it beats in vain. It cannot climb. It can only pass by doubling the huge buttresses and promontories. Sometimes it is flattened down to a shallow disk on the surface of the sea, spinning like a horizontal flywheel, dark, angry, furious, deadly, while

*A rod, a unit of length of 16.5 feet or 5.029 meters; 150 rods equals 2,475 feet or nearly half a mile.—Ed.

the sea birds congregate out of harm's way in the calm regions a few hundred feet above, and the sun looks serenely down on the black delirium beneath.

This was the case with the typhoon just referred to as having caught in its toils so many of the ships of our squadron on their way back from Japan. Some of the officers noticed that "even when the wind was piping loudest, when the water was whirled violently by in perfect sheets, the scud moved overhead at a remarkably slow rate, and the upper layer of clouds seemed scarcely to be stirred at all." On one of those grim nights, while our rolling ship was lying to off the chain of islands that stretches from Japan to Lew Chew, not daring to run through in such a tempest and on such imperfect charts, I remember how the moon struggled almost through the weltering haze and what a ghastly glare she cast on the boiling sea. Strange that a few hundred feet of altitude should make all the difference between a calm and a hurricane—between paradise and hell.

The prognostics of these storms are well fitted to inspire alarm. Nature is not uniform. A western tornado will sometimes burst upon its victims with little or no warning. But those that come in the daytime can frequently be seen at a distance making their lurid preparations. A writer in the signal service describes it thus—it is likely that he has seen one coming: "The first sign of a tornado is generally a tumultuous, strange appearance in the southwest;

and then the whirling funnel comes in sight writhing and swinging from side to side, now rising and again seeming to plunge down to the ground; its winds tear limbs from trees and roofs from houses, and suck them upwards with clouds of dust and debris. As it sweeps over a village, the houses on its path are not blown over, but exploded, and their walls fall outward on all sides. Heavy wagons, beams, and chains are all picked up and transported through the air. Lighter objects, such as boards, shingles, clothing, and papers, are often carried miles away before they fall."

Another observer gives a still more circumstantial account:[1] "Innumerable descriptions show that the cloud in the northwest is heavy, black, and comparatively slow in its movement, until struck by a light, rather smoky, and more rapidly moving cloud from the southwest. Then the clouds rush to a common center, and there is a violent conflict of currents, driving clouds in every direction, up and down, round and round. Clouds like great sheets of white smoke dash about in a frightful manner, with such unnatural velocity that the observer is often panic-stricken and flees to the nearest cellar for safety. Finally a black, threatening mass descends slowly toward the earth, whirling violently, but still manifesting confusion in form. This soon gives place to the peculiar funnel-like shape, with definite outline so well-known. It appears intensely black,

[1]*Popular Science Monthly,* xxviii, p. 313.

like coal smoke issuing from a locomotive, and its trunk-like form sometimes has a wrenching spiral motion, like a snake hung up by the head and writhing in agony. As white clouds approach and are drawn into the vortex, the funnel-shaped trunk sways like an elastic column. It sometimes rises, falls, and careens from side to side like a balloon. Branches and trunks of trees, rails, treetops, pieces of houses, straw, furniture, stoves, roofs, iron-work, lumber, and other debris are seen flying about in the central part of the cloud, but are gradually drawn upward and thrown out near the top, usually not until the storm has progressed a mile or two farther on from a given point. Dark masses of cloud are seen to shoot downward on either side of the funnel, to enter it just above the ground, and to apparently rush upward through the center and out at the top in a terrific manner. Sometimes the funnel pauses and whirls with apparently increased velocity, reducing everything to splinters, and leaving scarcely a vestige of a house or clump of trees, all being ground comparatively fine and carried away as chaff. The people at Westwood describe the roar of the tornado as having a peculiar hollow, humming sound. It somewhat resembles the rumbling of cars, or the booming of the sea. The sound is indescribable and unlike any other in nature. It is so loud that the falling of heavy trees against the side of a house and the crash of falling buildings are lost in the general roar."

The more formidable cyclones that ravage the deep usually send their dread heralds in advance. M. Reclus in describing their approach indulges in some vivid rhetoric. "Some days before the terrible hurricane is unchained, nature, already gloomy, and as if veiled, seems to anticipate a disaster. The little white clouds which float in the heights of air with the counter trade winds are hidden under a yellowish or dirty white vapor; the heavenly bodies are surrounded by vaguely iridescent halos and heavy layers of clouds, which in the evening present the most magnificent shadows of purple and of gold stretching far over the horizon, and the air is as stifling as if it came from the mouth of some great furnace. The cyclone, which already whirls in the upper regions, gradually approaches the surface of the ground or water. Torn fragments of reddish or black clouds are carried furiously along by the storm, which plunges and hurries through space; the column of mercury is wildly agitated in the barometer and sinks rapidly; the birds assemble as if to take counsel, then fly swiftly away so as to escape the tempest that pursues them. Soon a dark mass shows itself in the threatening part of the sky; this mass increases and spreads itself out, gradually covering the azure with a veil of a terrible darkness or a blood-colored hue. This is the cyclone, which fills and takes possession of its empire, twisting its immense spirals around the horizon. The roaring of the seas and skies succeeds to this awful silence."

These hurricanes have a will of their own, and revolve in opposite directions on opposite sides of the equator. In the southern hemisphere they wheel from left to right, like the hands of a watch; in the northern, from right to left. This is not their only motion. Occasionally one will spin on the same spot, like a top; but most of them, like the planets, not only revolve on their axis but at the same time travel in an orbit, sometimes with great velocity. The rate attained by the entire body of the storm varies from one mile per hour to forty, fifty, and even sixty. The distances traversed vary still more. A few hundred rods may exhaust the tornado. A few hundred miles would make a fair average for the cyclone.

Probably the most extensive track that has ever been traced and mapped was that of the great storm of 1885, which circumnavigated more than half the globe. It was generated near the southern coast of China in the latter part of September, "passed over Japan and the Aleutian archipelago, and entered the United States on 10 October. Crossing the Rocky Mountain range it proceeded through the northern states and Canada to Labrador and Davis Strait. In the Atlantic it was joined on the eighteenth by another disturbance which had come up from the Atlantic tropics, the junction of the two being followed by a cessation of progressive movement from the nineteenth to the twenty-fifth. During this period a severe gale that passed along the southern counties of England on the morning of the twenty-fourth—a storm the forecasting of which was shown to be impossible—was formed. Following in the wake of this storm, the parent cyclone reached the French coast on the twenty-seventh, its advent being marked by violent gales and extensive floods over the whole of western and central Europe and Algeria. Passing through France and the Netherlands, the disturbance showed signs of exhaustion, and on 1 November, in the Baltic, it quietly dispersed, after accomplishing a journey of more than sixteen thousand miles in thirty-six days."[2]

The speed with which these portents travel along the surface is slow compared with their frightful gyrations on their own axis; a velocity which hurls weighty masses out of their path with the force of dynamite. In the hurricane of August 1837, at St. Thomas,* an eyewitness writes, "The fort at the entrance of the harbor is leveled with the foundation and the twenty-four pounders thrown down; it looks as if it had been battered to pieces by cannon shot. . . . One fine American ship, five hundred tons, was driven on shore near the citadel, and in an hour nothing could be seen of her but a few timbers." In the Iowa cyclone of 1882, trees, cattle, hu-

[2]*Popular Science Monthly*, April, 1886, p. 857.

*Presumably St. Thomas in the Virgin Islands of the West Indies, a United States possession today, as purchased from Denmark in 1917.—Ed.

man beings, even houses, were sucked up into the enormous spirals, whisked through the air, and then dashed to atoms. This was the storm that was so fatal to the institution at Grinnell.* Usually colleges investigate phenomena; this phenomenon investigated the college, and it did it with a scientific thoroughness that left nothing more to be further analyzed.

I have spoken of an "axis." An axis of course there is; but around it lies a central space of calms, which may be rods or even miles in diameter. The typhoon center is greatly dreaded by the navigator. A ship caught within the deadly enclosure wallows unmanageably in a tumbling sea and inside a cylinder of wind whose walls are whirling with a frightful speed. Violent squalls and waterspouts are sent tearing off from the revolving walls, and go thundering to and fro within the cylinder like a bedlam of demons.

In one of our many visits to Hong Kong, an English man-of-war came into port which had undergone a novel experience. In crossing the Indian Ocean she found a typhoon was making the same trip just north of her and about parallel with her own course. Her plucky commander was of an inquiring turn of mind and thought his ugly neighbor would bear investigation. He accordingly battened down his hatches and sailed in and out of the storm three times for the purpose of determining its size

*Iowa's Grinnell College.–Ed.

and course and verifying the direction and force of the wind. Then he hove to and waited, and when at a safe distance sailed across its wake. There he found a big ship over which the center had passed, waterlogged, dismasted, and terribly mangled in the mighty struggle. He had the happiness of picking off her crew before she went down.

Of all the apparatus of havoc that belongs to the hurricane, there is one more to be noted which is peculiarly fatal. It is the storm wave. The hurricane not only draws into its vortex the winds and lightnings and clouds; it sucks in the sea also and lifts a disk of water above the general level of the ocean almost as broad as its own diameter. This enormous tidal wave does not revolve with the wind at all, but is drawn forward and keeps pace with it. Like a murderous slave it does the bidding of the typhoon, and is ready to engulf fleets, submerge islands, demolish towns, desolate anything that may lie in its track. Read the list of hurricanes that have ravaged the West Indies and our own southern coast, from the first one noted by Columbus down to this present year of grace. In many cases the storm has carried with it appalling inundations that have buried villages and strewn the wrecks of vessels far inland.

In October 1864, this tempest-wave raised the Hoogly twenty-two feet for many miles above Calcutta, sweeping banks and islands with a fatal flood. A cyclone that struck the southern coast of India in

1789 led in its train three storm-waves that buried a city of thirty thousand inhabitants and lifted a whole fleet of vessels far up on the shore. In a similar catastrophe in 1876, which broke without warning in the night, three large islands and many smaller ones off the mouth of the Ganges were buried by a wave twenty feet deep, and more than two hundred fifty thousand hapless beings were swept into the sea. During a typhoon that passed over Kobe, Japan, in July 1871, scores of ships and junks were carried into the fields and forests far beyond the reach of the highest tides. In one of the violent hurricanes of the West Indies, the waves broke on the northern shores of the Barbados seventy-two feet above the mean level.

The memorable storm of October 1780 has been known as the most terrible cyclone of modern times. The ravages of its tidal wave were almost as destructive as those of the tempest itself. This frightful convulsion hurled its weight upon the hapless islands and fleets in its way more like an avalanche of the ocean than a mere tempest. It spared nothing. Squadrons were crushed like egg-shells and sent to the bottom with all on board. An English fleet at anchor off St. Lucia went down on the spot. A French convoy with five thousand troops on board, several men-of-war on their way home, and a large number of merchantmen trading among the islands, were overtaken and sunk with their crews. Cities and plantations were ravaged as terribly as the deep. On the various islands nearly twenty thousand people were crushed under the wreck of their homes, or mangled by the countless missiles flying through the air, or swept off by the tidal wave.

A less extensive hurricane, but almost equally destructive, fell upon the southern coast of China in the autumn of 1874. Hong Kong was almost torn to pieces. Every vessel in the harbor or on the coast was crippled or sunk, and some eight thousand lives were lost. An officer of the Pacific mail steamer *Alaska* saw a fleet of more than one hundred Chinese junks founder all at once. The *Alaska* herself was driven on shore. Macao, seventy miles west, fared still worse. The storm obliterated whole streets and piled them with blocking ruins. To add to its horrors a band of pirates fired the city for purposes of plunder and seven hundred houses were consumed. Every vessel, foreign or native, was destroyed. Ten thousand lives were lost; and long before the dead could be disentangled for burial, the air became loaded with pestilence, and a wholesale cremation was ordered. The destruction of property reached a total of millions.

I trust the reader is in a forgiving mood, and our long delay in reaching this particular typhoon will be condoned. There is I believe a melancholy fascination about these grim tragedies of the sea; and I have gathered a few of the sad facts that demonstrate the power and the ferocity of this "sleeping giant" when it wakes in his wrath, creating havoc.

The ninth of October was creeping on. For some days the weather had been ugly and threatening. Somewhere a storm was mustering for the fray, and "Brooding its dreamy thunders far aloof."

The barometer fluttered for a day or two and then began to sink. The sky looked wicked. The wind was blowing hard and increasing. Sail had been gradually reduced. The waves had worked themselves into a most uncomfortable ferment. "Rocked in the cradle of the deep" is very romantic when you sing it, but not so nice when the cradle breaks your head and threatens to pitch you out. The timbers moaned and creaked, and the spars aloft groaned with the extra pressure when some deeper lurch swept them roaring back against the blast. I do not know a sound more dismal or ominous than the sepulchral tones wrung from the very fiber of the ship as she staggers reluctantly onward to meet the coming storm, perhaps to meet her doom. She seems to be groaning her own requiem beforehand.

When a tempest is on hand, sailors like to make all snug alow and aloft. Seamanship requires it. So does safety. The sailor is not the reckless being you think him when you see him at work astride a yard-arm, or standing on a rope reefing topsails seventy-five feet in the air. He is a prehensile animal, and has methods of clinging that are not recognized in common philosophy. By noon we were in a state of uncomfortable preparation; royal and topgallant yards and masts sent down and stowed on deck; spare spars and boats made fast with extra lanyards; guns secured with double lashings; hatches battened down, and life-lines stretched along the decks.*

A man-of-war is built for offensive warfare; but in an encounter with a tempest she is wholly on the defensive. She cannot attack the storm, it is the storm that attacks her. She cannot even strike back. There is no brilliant maneuver with which she can flank her omnipresent antagonist. Her petty array of battery, pikes, carbines, and cutlasses, with which she plays battle with other toy ships like herself, are worse than useless in the presence of a foe that scours around the horizon, skirmishes at her from invisible distances, blinds her with Egyptian darkness, crazes her with a savage drunken sea, and gathering its forces into successive paroxysms of wrath swoops down upon her with the weight and plunge of half the heavens falling. Then her battery is her deadliest burden, and her sharpest weapons make her only a more bristling target for the lightnings. She cannot screen herself. She cannot ward off the pitiless blows. She can only lie there on the devilish sea and take unresisting all the fury and ferocity with which her grim adversary can belabor

*A full-rigged ship carried a lower, topsail, topgallant, royal, and sometimes a skysail, yard, on each mast. The topsail was usually double.—Ed.

her. The "Thing" that was coming was evidently a cyclone or, in the vernacular of the East, a typhoon. Either term is sufficiently hideous to anyone whose judgment of the sign is at all guided by his experience of the thing signified.

With the data at hand it would not be easy to determine where this particular hurricane originated, or in the throes of what atmospheric convulsion it may have been brought to the agony of birth. There was a villainous gale the same day at Madras, with a fearful score of wrecks and lives; but that was two thousand miles to the west of us, and our assailant came from the area of southeast. The October mail steamer was badly damaged by a typhoon a few days before us in nearly the same spot, but that storm had vanished; thus ours could not have been its residuum. The *Sobrao*, a Portuguese ship, was caught in a typhoon off the Bashees which lasted ten days, and finally, mangled, dismasted, and utterly exhausted, she held together long enough for an American barque to pick off her crew, then sullenly gave up the fight and went down. This was two days before our hurricane and seven hundred or eight hundred miles to the east. It is possible that the vortex in which we were entrapped may have been an eddy sent tearing off from this larger sphere. If so, its path must have been a curve cutting diagonally across Luzon or down its western shores before it struck off over the seas in quest of other prey. The weather record of Manila for the autumn of 1852, if our Filipino friends kept such records then, would easily determine.

We never knew what other havoc it may have inflicted, with the single exception of one comrade in distress, an English ship that started for California and had the ill luck to be beset by three cyclones in succession. The last of the three was ours, and it well nigh finished her. It was "too much typhoon," as our Celestial friends admitted; and in process of time she came limping back into Hong Kong, halt, crippled, masts gone, bulwarks and everything else swept clean with the deck from forecastle to cabin. Logically she ought to have gone to the bottom; but her three tormentors were considerate enough not to come all at once. It was an unusually bad season. Many were the giant storms that stalked over the waves and many the craft that attempted to run the gauntlet. Some succeeded and escaped into more amiable seas; some were baffled and put back for help; and some left their mangled ribs to garnish the reefs, or vanished in the still depths where the storms send their victims and plunder but can never go themselves.

We had been all day standing out to the northward and eastward on the port tack, with the wind from the northward and westward. The farther we got, the more violent was the gale and the heavier the sea. No wonder, for we were plunging straight into the storm. The path of the cyclone was just to the north of us. It was crossing the China Sea on a west-nor'west course. We entered its southwest quarter, and were therefore heading straight for its center nearly all the afternoon. Any East Indian navigator who may chance to read this account would say that we were on the wrong tack. Yes, we were; but to a ship on a lee shore, Hobson's choice may be the only one open. Our position at noon that day was latitude 17° 41', longitude 110° 34', southeast of Gaalong Bay. It had been the captain's intention to run in, but the wind was contrary, in every sense of the term, and the coveted shelter of Gaalong was impossible. Our special danger was from the Paracels—an immense tract of reefs and shoals something like a hundred square miles, without an island or rock above the level of the sea on which a poor waif might find refuge in case he outlived the boiling surge and the tearing coral. We were just to windward of this sunken trap.

With the Paracels on one side and a typhoon on the other, it was worse than being caught "between the devil and the deep sea." It was not inspiring to reflect that if we did not founder before reaching it we might go smashing upon it at any moment. In the desperate effort to claw off, the ship was staggering under a press of canvas which otherwise she would not have dared to carry. The farther out we got, the more furious and brutal the sea. A stunning blow from the crest of a wave dashed in upon the starboard head;* the decks had long been flooded.

*Starboard head, one of the ship's water closets.—Ed.

At every lurch, mountains of brine tumbled on board. Sail had been gradually reduced to foresail and main topsail, both close-reefed,* with main try-sail and fore storm-staysail. But the violence of the wind, instead of driving her forward, pressed her over almost on her beam ends, and she was drifting bodily to leeward. But that way lay the Paracels. That would not do. The canvas must come off.

Meanwhile all hands on deck; all the officers were summoned to the cabin. The first lieutenant had taken the deck. His stentorian voice could roar like a bull of Bashan; but in the fury of the storm even his voice could not be heard six inches from his lips. The orders were given in the cabin and were carried forward among the men by the other officers who picked their way desperately along the life lines. It is a serious job to shorten sail in a hurricane; commonly the hurricane does not wait for you but does it itself. The first rope started might take the masts out of her. But there was no alternative. And after a hard fight of two hours with the whole crew at the ropes, the poor *Saratoga* was lying under bare poles, wallowing, pitching, rolling, plunging, almost sinking in the pitiless sea; the foresail clewed up and stowed after a fashion, the storm-staysail blown out of the bolt-ropes, the try-sail ripped into shreds and wound in all impossible ways about the main shrouds and running rigging.

*Close-reefed sails have had their areas reduced to lessen the wind's impact.–Ed.

The main topsail gave the poor fellows the toughest work and the greatest danger. By superhuman effort it was clewed up, and the boatswain, a powerfully muscular man, led the crew of maintopmen up to furl it. He managed to crawl into the slings of the yard, but not a man would follow him. Brave as they were, the scene was enough to defy human power. The yard, though of course down on the cap, was still seventy-five feet and more from the deck. The great sail was flapping and writhing and tugging like a Titan, and threatened to rip yard and all into the sea. The mast whirled in giddy circles, sometimes dipping the yardarms in the foam; and with such sudden and furious jerks that it required all one's strength to hold on and keep from being flung overboard. The air was full of driving scud and black as pitch. The wind scooped off the tops of the waves and sent them hissing through the rigging with the force of a chain shot. And the ghastly phosphorescence of the sea as it boiled around the ship and through the broken ports and then over hammock nettings cast a deathly glare over the scene that served to make the darkness visible. The men crept down and abandoned the sail to its fate. It had four reefs in it, and these held; but all below them was stripped into ragged ribbons. Next morning the poor topsail, which was nearly new, was a curiosity fit for a museum.

All this time we were heading to the northward and eastward on the port tack. It was certain that the Paracels were right under our lee; how near, we could only conjecture. And though we were forging slowly ahead, yet we were drifting very much faster toward those fatal rocks. It was decided to get the ship about if possible, set some patch of canvas that might perhaps hold, and run her out into wider sea room. Then we could resume that port tack whenever the shift of wind should indicate that the storm had traveled far enough to bring us out of its southwestern quarter into the southeastern. Any shipmaster will understand how a vessel caught in a typhoon to windward of the Paracels and entering it from the south would find the port tack the wrong one to get into the storm and the right one to get out of it.

With infinite difficulty and risk, the ship was got round on the starboard tack and headed about southwest. She met her new course with a frightful lurch and then a bound and plunge as if determined to do her best. But it was asking too much. She made no headway, and those dread rocks, like a magnet, were dragging her to leeward as fast as before. Three or four hours must settle our fate. We watched the barometer. Will it never stop falling? Does it mean that we are nearing the center? Shall we go down in that horrible vortex? Or will the storm keep us up until it can dash us on those ghastly reefs? If the cyclone is of great diameter, or is passing slowly, the wind must hold from the same quarter for a long time and there will be no escaping the shoals. Better be on the port tack. That might give us a ghost of a chance. Preparations were made accordingly for wearing ship.* But by this time she had become quite unmanageable. In that weltering mob of a sea, with enormous pyramids of black water rushing at her from all directions at once, half submerging her and then in the next breath pitching her out on the tip of a roaring billow, she would not mind her helm, nor pay the least attention to any of the more common arts of seamanship.

As a last resort a desperate experiment was tried, which I had read of but had never expected to witness. The ship was under bare poles and not a rag of canvas could live on her for a moment. With an immense deal of persuasion, some of it more force than suasion, a hundred or more of the men were driven into the weather fore rigging from twenty to fifty feet above deck, where they formed a dense mass against which the hurricane drove with tremendous pressure. This was attempted by a man-of-war caught in the disastrous hurricane at Samoa in 1889; in this case the men being massed in the mizzen shrouds instead of the fore.

I have often thought of those men thus hung in mid air, and congratulated myself that it was not

*The maneuver of wearing ship, an extremely hazardous undertaking under such circumstances as Sewall describes, changes a vessel's heading from one tack close-hauled on the wind to another by putting up or redirecting the helm or tiller and, hence, the rudder.—Ed.

one of the duties of a captain's clerk to be among them. Drenched with the salt spray, benumbed, yet clinging like death to the slippery shrouds, whirled and jerked through the air by the writhing ship beneath, swept over the boiling caldron of waters now on the one side and the next instant on the other, it was a miracle that they were not every man of them snapped off and shot headlong into the sea; and all the while the black night made lurid and infernal by the phosphorescent foam, and the elements roaring together with a din more deafening and horrible than 40 million parks of artillery and as many more locomotives, all thundering, howling, booming, and screeching at once. While these poor fellows were hanging on for dear life in the fore shrouds, other men were stationed with axes to cut away the mizzenmast. The helm was put hard up. But the poor ship, lacerated and exhausted, seemed unable to make any further effort and lay helplessly wallowing and tumbling like a log. A desperate half-hour had passed since the men crept into the rigging. It seemed a week. The order was on the lips of the first lieutenant to cut away, when at last as if awaking to the situation and rousing from some dreadful swoon, she showed signs of returning life. She began to feel her helm and the terrific pressure of the wind on that black swarm in the fore rigging, and slowly and painfully began to pay off. It was a perilous moment as she swung round into the trough of the sea. Will she live through it? More likely she will roll herself under and go down. We braced ourselves and held our breath. Then both batteries went under, as indeed they had been doing all the evening. But there was good stuff in her yet.

As she came to her course, with a few tremendous lurches she shook herself clear of the mountains of water on her decks and rose heavily and wearily on the next wave. Once fairly round on the port tack it was found that the change had come that the far-seeing barometer had already predicted. The wind was hauling to the westward. This meant that the center of the storm was directly north of us and was rapidly passing. It meant also that we were not to leave our bones on the Paracels. As it proved, the evolution had been performed under the fiercest blast we had that night. It was nine o'clock when we wore ship. The storm continued to rage with fury, but the squalls came less frequently and were less spiteful. By midnight it had so far spent itself that it was safe to begin to make sail. With the close-reefed foresail on her again she was steadier, and, crippled as she was, did her best to crawl out of the dread neighborhood in which she had so nearly met her doom. What that doom would have been you can imagine from the memory of scores of proud ships that have sailed out on the mysterious sea, from which no tidings have ever come back to the wives and mothers who watched and wept and prayed. Or if the grim Paracels had been our sepulchre, death would have been still more tragic. There are no islands in that submerged continent of graves; no friendly strand on which a drowning waif might possibly be cast; nothing but murderous ledges and wild tearing coral reefs. Had the *Saratoga* struck there, five minutes would have sufficed to rend ship and crew into shreds and scatter them throughout miles of quite angry surf.

The next morning was a peaceful Sabbath. When I went on deck at six bells, the sun was shining. The sea had quieted down, and a languid breeze was wafting us gently along; sky and ocean demurely innocent–apparently no recollection of the wild orgies of the night before. The morning watch was sending down the fragments of split sails and bending others in their stead. The decks were still lumbered with debris and everything drenched and soaked. You may remember how Bessus, the poltroon in one of Beaumont and Fletcher's plays, described his memorable drubbing: "I think I have been cudgelled by all nations, and almost all religions." If our poor old belabored craft could have put herself into rhetoric, that is doubtless the way in which she would have expressed her feelings. Three boats were missing, torn away davits and all. Spare spars in the main chains were gone, ports smashed in, and loads of the smaller deck furniture, battle-axes, cutlasses, handspikes, life buoys, halyard racks, and the like, washed overboard. During the night the spanker boom had got adrift and taken command of the poop, sweeping it clean of everything; and cutting up the heavy iron rail on both sides had twirled it into the mizzen rigging like so much wire.

There was no loss of life. Many of the crew were half drowned in the scuppers, or cut and bruised as they were swept to and fro across the decks in avalanches of waves, ropes, spars, men, and everything movable in a jumble together. But the "Thing" was passed, and we had come out alive. It was an immense satisfaction to find that we were still on top of the ocean instead of the ocean on top of us. A week sufficed to repair damages and make things shipshape. And we started up the seas again to renew our quest of pirates and glory.

Neither glory nor pirates were to be had for the asking. But we had the luck to encounter one episode that is pleasant to remember. One forenoon, a fortnight after our mauling by the tempest, the lookout at the masthead sung out, "Sail ho!" It was but a speck on the distant waves, perhaps a derelict, or a tangle of jetsam from some foundering bark. But as we approached we could see something moving on board. It proved to be a Chinese fishing boat, dismasted in a typhoon three days after ours. The wretched survivors were waving frantic signals of distress. We sent a boat and took them off. For nearly a fortnight they had been drifting about on the waves, provisions gone, and nothing left but to surrender to starvation or the merciless sea. They were helped on board, six gaunt skeletons; and the first thing they did was to drop on their knees and knock their foreheads on the deck, worshiping officers and crew alike for rescuing them from death. I never saw a more pathetic sight. The next thing was to turn them over to the medical department for such mild nutrition as would save them from starving. Then we went to quarters, cast loose the guns, and began blazing away at the dismasted junk in order to sink her out of the way of passing ships. But somehow the balls were contrary; the sea was rough, and she got only four shots out of a whole broadside. As she did not seem disposed to be good and go to the bottom, another boat was sent to set her on fire. We filled away and left her blazing astern.

Another week and our time was up. We plodded our way back to the old berth, and without pirates, without glory, but with a lot of experience, we came to anchor as usual in Macao roads.

V

The Scourge of the Eastern Seas

IF WE DID not catch any pirates in that dismal cruise, we can pursue them through another chapter and perhaps may overtake some of them yet. It is much easier to catch them on paper than on the high seas.[1]

If any part of the world might seem to have been originally designed for a pirates' paradise, the southern coast of China is the place. Fringed with capes, beaded with islands of every size and shape, pierced by estuaries made up of numberless winding channels, it opens to the sea-rover countless coves and pockets and watery labyrinths, for lying in ambush or hiding from pursuit. One of the wide-spread groups of islands through whose tortuous passages the Canton River finds its way to the sea

[1]The chief authorities for the facts given in this chapter are various volumes of the *Chinese Repository* and of the *Asiatic Journal*; S. Wells Williams, *The Middle Kingdom*; Du Halde, *General History of China*; Guillemard, *Australasia*; also from Wallace's, *Australasia*; Fortune, *Residence Among the Chinese*; Downing, *Fanqui in China*; Forbes, *Five Years in China*; St. John, *The Wild Coasts of Nipon*; Yung-lun-yuen, *History of the Pirates who infested the China Sea from 1807 to 1810*, translated by Charles Friedrich Newman; and my own manuscript diary of four years on the East India station. Many writers on oriental topics and books of travel have been consulted.

has been the scene of so many of these tragedies that it has richly earned its sinister title: the Ladrones (Robbers).* Ever since primeval commerce began to creep along the shores of the great empire, it has doubtless had its bloody parasites. The lonely trader and the clumsy fleet have had to reckon with this ever-present menace as one of the risks of the voyage. It was never certain from behind what headland or out of what lagoon might issue at any moment a pack of these ocean wolves. If departing voyagers never returned, it was sometimes the typhoons and sometimes the pirates. Dead men tell no tales.

It is easy to cover with facile phrase the long and painful evolution of the centuries, especially the slow-moving cycles of Cathay. It is not so easy to fill in the picture with the actual details; to imagine the growing commerce and the growing piracy that preyed upon it; to portray the long ages of sorrow on the sea—first the stealthy surprise, the sharp attack, the vain attempt to flee, the desperate stand at bay, the fight for life, the brutish yells, the cry for mercy, the ghastly silence that settles on the slippery decks as the butchers leisurely proceed to rifle their prey. What myriads of tragedies like this have been enacted far back in the dim primeval, while the Celestial Empire has been slowly emerging

*As piracy is the theme of this chapter, the Ladrones (Robbers) Islands, lying just off the Canton or Pearl River, were aptly named.—Ed.

Chinese Junks on the Canton River, April 1853

Courtesy The Beverly R. Robinson Collection, United States Naval Academy Museum, Annapolis, Maryland

from savagery into national life, no chronicler has told. But at least it was a process of martial training. As Chinese commerce has run the gauntlet and fought its way into existence, it has developed in its own mariners, and in their assailants as well, those qualities of courage, hardihood, and grit which the Western world could but admire in the brave fellows of the Yalu fight in 1894.* The handling of the *Ting Yuen* and the *Chen Yuen*, especially in the latter part of the action, affords ample proof of the pluck of the Chinese man-of-war's man when his blood is up.

The victory fell to Japan; but history will award to the Admiral Ting Ju Chang and his men the credit due to their daring and skill. They fought for their country against what they believed to be unjust usurpation; and, as one reads of their deeds of valor, it is easy to imagine that in the veins of some of those warriors ran the blood of generations of old-time buccaneers. The annals of Chinese piracy have not wholly faded into oblivion. Some epochs in its history are familiar to those students who have a fancy for mousing about in the unbeaten tracks of oriental life. A glimpse at the *modus operandi* will help to develop an intelligent appreciation of these gruesome records. A few modern samples will suffice.

The year before our futile quest for these various

*Sewall refers to a naval battle off the Yalu River in the Sino-Japanese War of 1894–95.—Ed.

gentlemen of the high seas as narrated in the last chapter, Captain Massie of the steamship H. B. M. *Cleopatra*[*] sent out a boat expedition among the islands, which, after a running fight of five hours, captured three eighteen-gun lorchas; and yet two months afterward, on about the same cruising ground, the *Brillante* was cut off by free-booters, plundered of a large amount of treasure, the crew massacred, and the ship scuttled and sunk. In March 1853, her majesty's steam-sloop *Hermes* came upon the scent of a whole squadron a little way up the coast. After a hot pursuit, the outlaws turned at bay and defended themselves with savage ferocity. But they were no match for British guns and steam. The *Hermes* avenged some of their villainies by sending four junks to the bottom and towing three more as prizes back to Hong Kong.

In the summer of 1835 there came limping into Hong Kong harbor a much-abused hulk whose misadventures inspired sympathy wherever her pitiful story came to be known. It was the English barque *Troughton* from Singapore. First of all, she encountered a typhoon that did not leave her until her masts were wrenched out of her and her bulwarks were torn off clean with the decks. Her exhausted crew managed to keep her afloat with the pumps and, rigging a sail on a jury-mast, were

*In Queen Victoria's time, H.B.M. signified Her Britannic Majesty, a prefix in this instance before the name of a vessel of the Royal Navy; abbreviation later changed to H.M.S.–Ed.

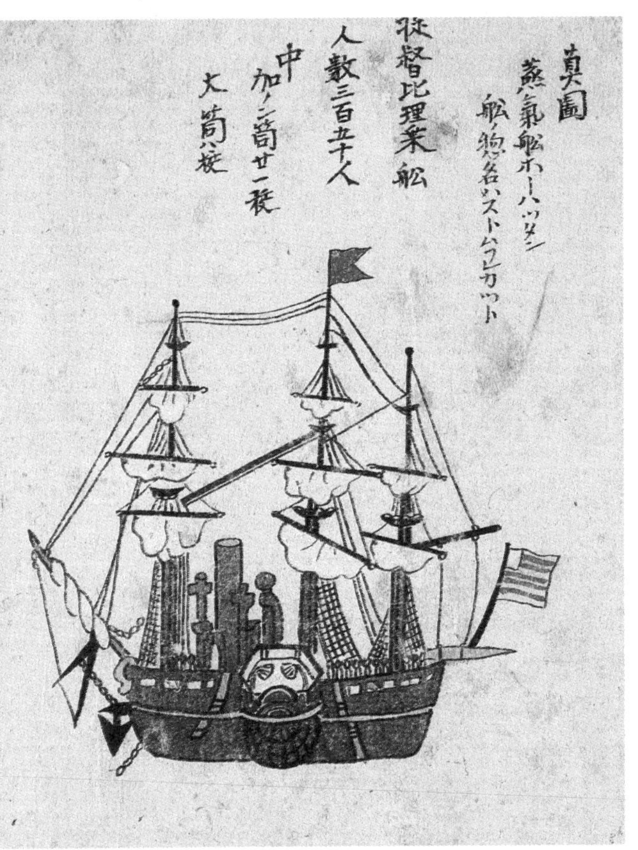

The Steamship Powhatan; *from the Black Ship Scroll*

Courtesy Honolulu Academy of Arts

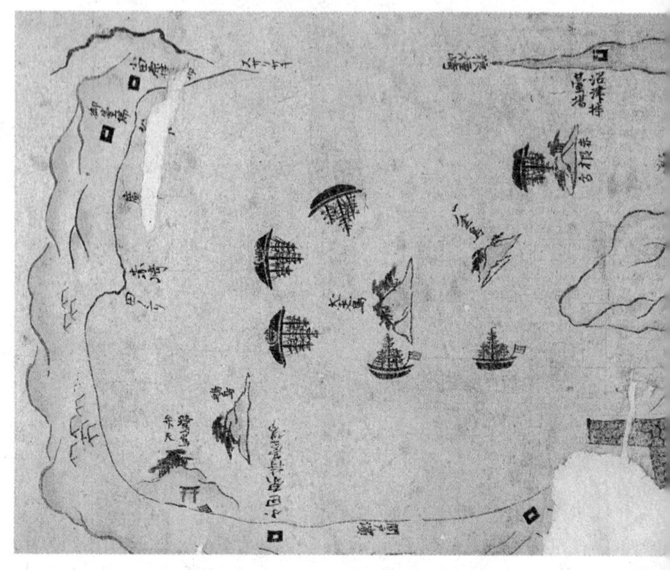

Map of Shimoda harbor; the town lies at the lower right—at anch
are six ships from Perry's squadron; from the Black Ship Scroll

Courtesy Honolulu Academy of Arts

EACH MAP in our Historical Atlas depicts the world in the mid 1800s—the time John Sewall spent aboard U.S.S. *Saratoga* and throughout Commodore Matthew Calbraith Perry's voyages that culminated in the opening of Japan.

The four-color illustrations in this section are from *Visit of American Ships to Shimoda Harbor, Kaei V (1853) with Commodore Perry, Officers and Men, etc.*, a handscroll (commonly referred to as the Black Ship Scroll). Dating from 1853, the scroll is in the collection of the Honolulu Academy of Arts (a gift of Mrs. Walter F. Dillingham in memory of Alice Perry Grew).

The Guide to Place Names lists place names and spellings from the mid nineteenth century with updates to current spellings and usage. Information, such as current ownership and/or helpful locational data, is printed in brackets [ ].

THE PUBLISHERS

ATLAS

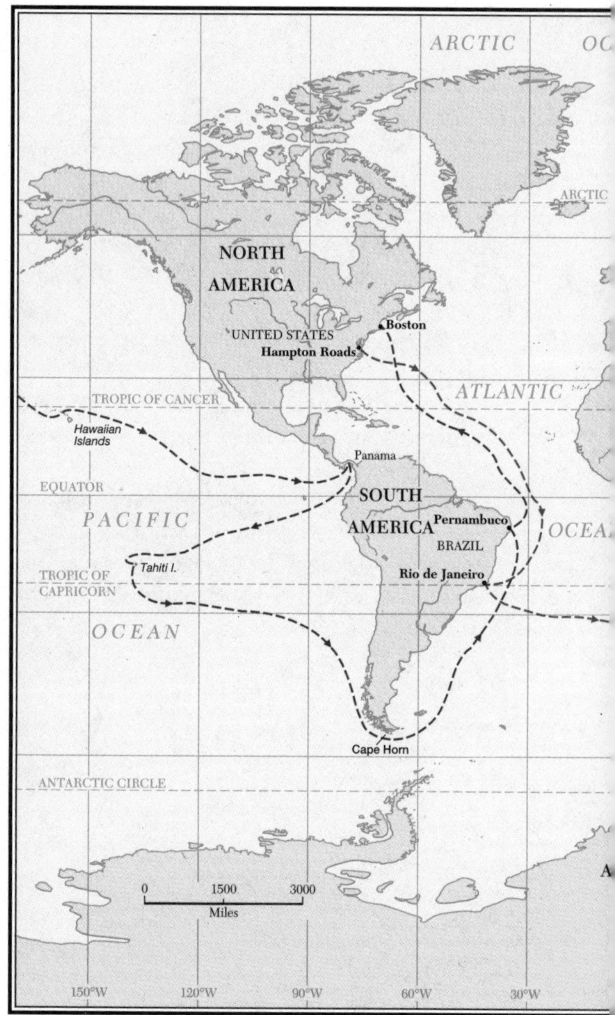
ARCTIC
OC
ARCTIC
NORTH
AMERICA
UNITED STATES
Boston
Hampton Roads
TROPIC OF CANCER
ATLANTIC
Hawaiian
Islands
Panama
EQUATOR
SOUTH
AMERICA
PACIFIC
Pernambuco
BRAZIL
OCEA
Tahiti I.
TROPIC OF
CAPRICORN
Rio de Janeiro
OCEAN
Cape Horn
ANTARCTIC CIRCLE
0
1500
3000
Miles
150°W
120°W
90°W
60°W
30°W

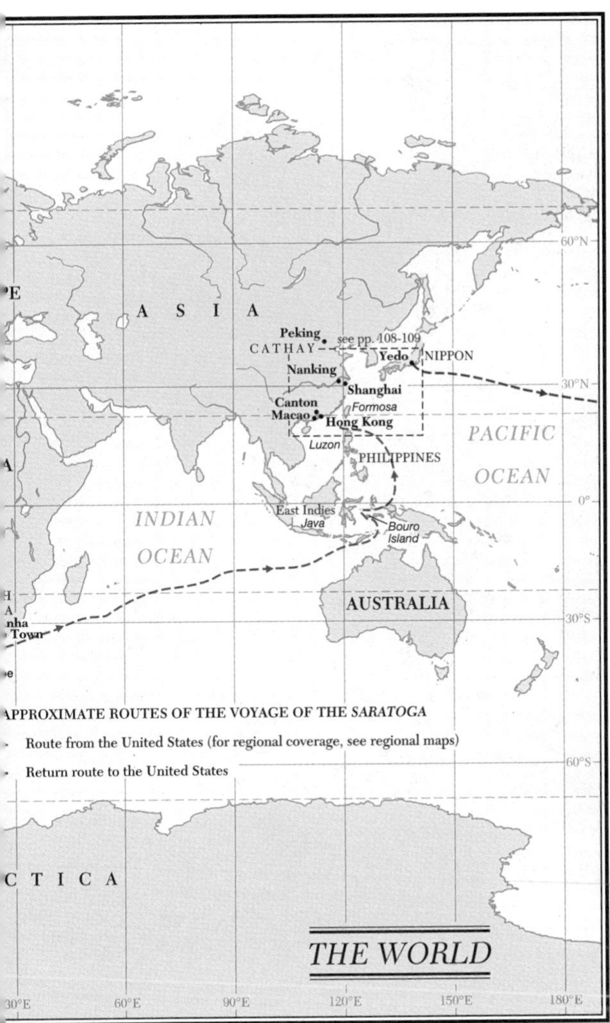
ASIA
Peking
see pp. 108-109
CATHAY
Yedo
NIPPON
Nanking
Shanghai
Canton
Macao
Formosa
Hong Kong
Luzon
PHILIPPINES
PACIFIC
OCEAN
INDIAN
OCEAN
East Indies
Java
Bouro
Island
AUSTRALIA
60°N
30°N
0°
30°S
60°S
APPROXIMATE ROUTES OF THE VOYAGE OF THE SARATOGA
Route from the United States (for regional coverage, see regional maps)
Return route to the United States
CTICA
THE WORLD
30°E
60°E
90°E
120°E
150°E
180°E

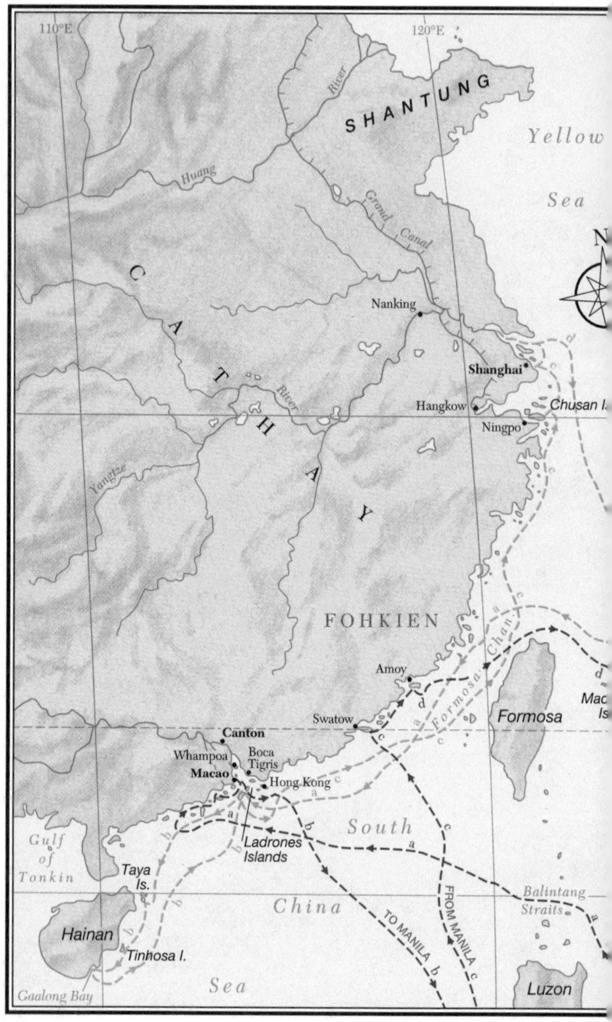

110°E
120°E
SHANTUNG
Yellow
Sea
River
Huang
Grand
Canal
C A T H A Y
Nanking
Shanghai
Hangkow
Chusan I.
Ningpo
River
Yangtze
FOHKIEN
Formosa Chan.
Amoy
Swatow
Formosa
Canton
Whampoa
Boca
Tigris
Macao
Hong Kong
South
Gulf
of
Tonkin
Ladrones
Islands
Taya
Is.
China
Balintang
Straits
Hainan
Tinhosa I.
TO MANILA
FROM MANILA
Sea
Gaalong Bay
Luzon

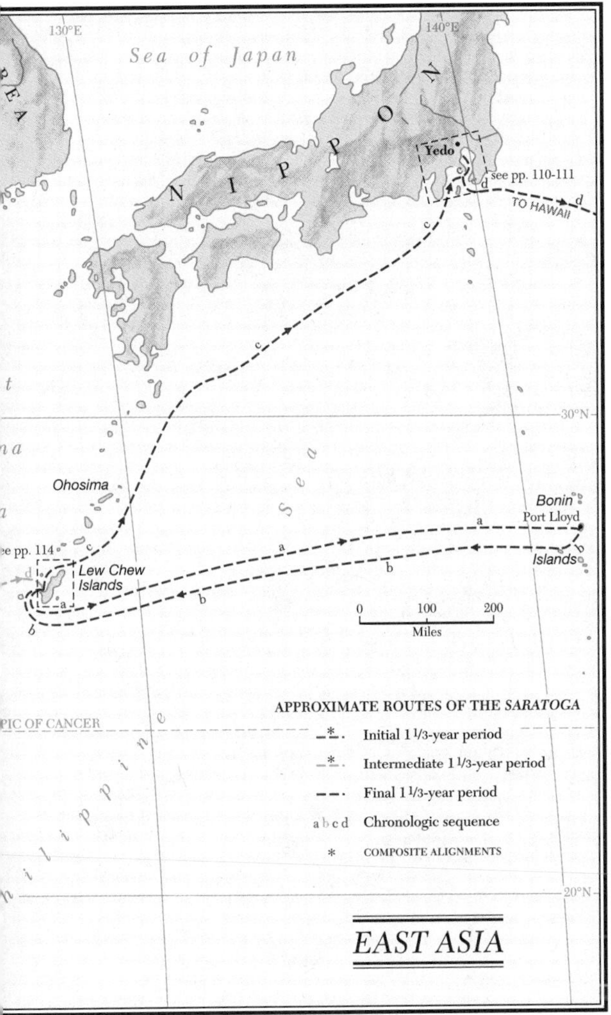
130°E
140°E
Sea of Japan
NIPPON
Yedo
see pp. 110-111
TO HAWAII
30°N
Ohosima
Bonin
Port Lloyd
Islands
see pp. 114
Lew Chew
Islands
0
100
200
Miles
APPROXIMATE ROUTES OF THE *SARATOGA*
Initial 1 1/3-year period
Intermediate 1 1/3-year period
Final 1 1/3-year period
a b c d Chronologic sequence
* COMPOSITE ALIGNMENTS
TROPIC OF CANCER
20°N
EAST ASIA

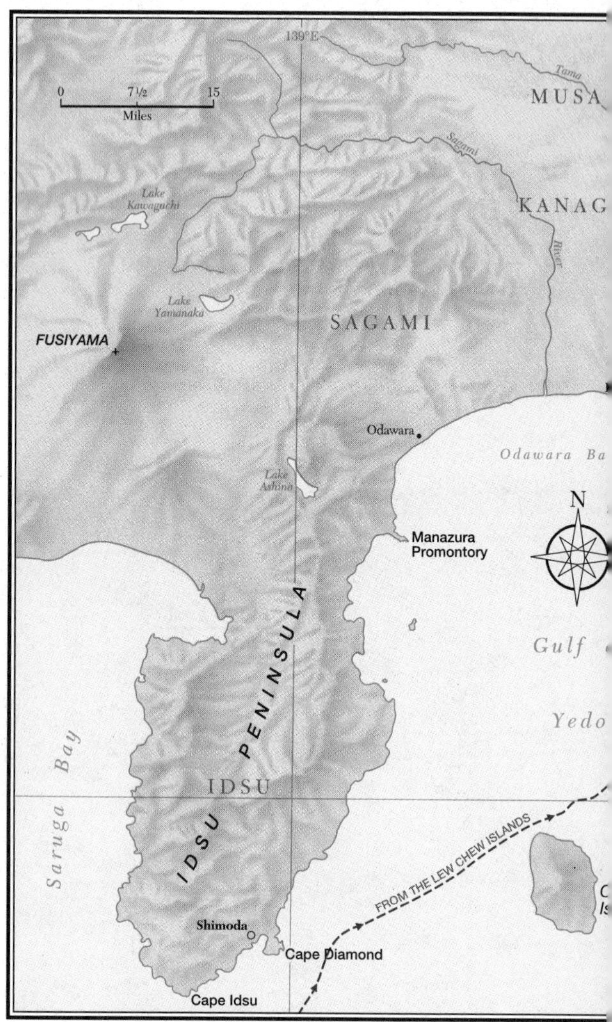
139°E
0
7½
15
Miles
Tama
MUSA
Sagami
KANAG
Lake
Kawaguchi
River
Lake
Yamanaka
SAGAMI
FUSIYAMA
Odawara
Odawara Ba
Lake
Ashino
N
Manazura
Promontory
IDSU PENINSULA
Gulf
Yedo
Saruga Bay
IDSU
FROM THE LEW CHEW ISLANDS
Shimoda
Cape Diamond
Cape Idsu

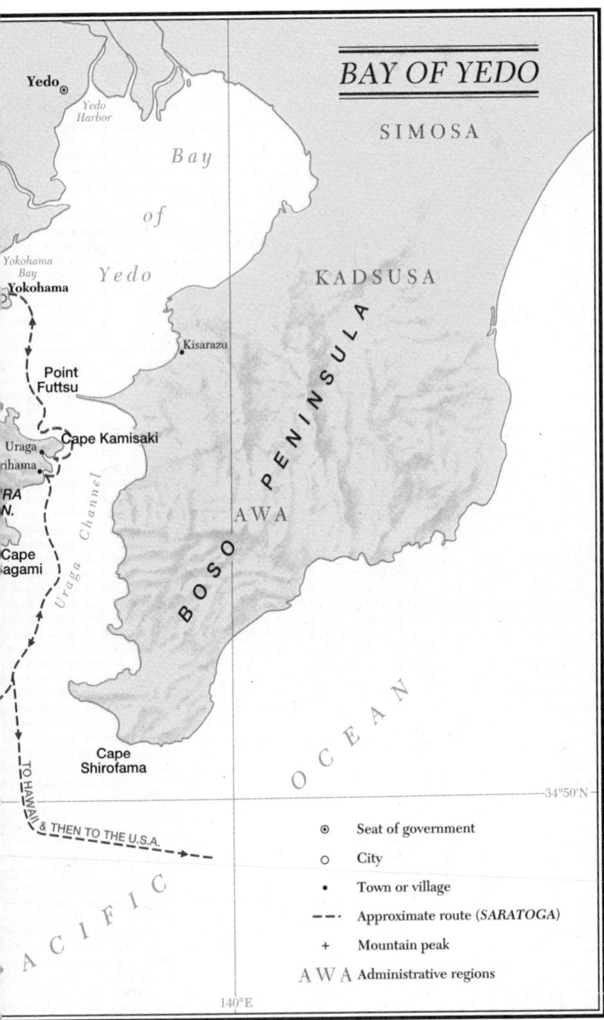
BAY OF YEDO
SIMOSA
Yedo
Yedo Harbor
Bay of Yedo
Yokohama Bay
Yokohama
KADSUSA
BOSO PENINSULA
Kisarazu
Point Futtsu
Cape Kamisaki
Uraga
Uraga Channel
AWA
Cape Shirofama
OCEAN
PACIFIC
TO HAWAII & THEN TO THE U.S.A.
34°50'N
140°E
Seat of government
City
Town or village
Approximate route (SARATOGA)
Mountain peak
AWA Administrative regions

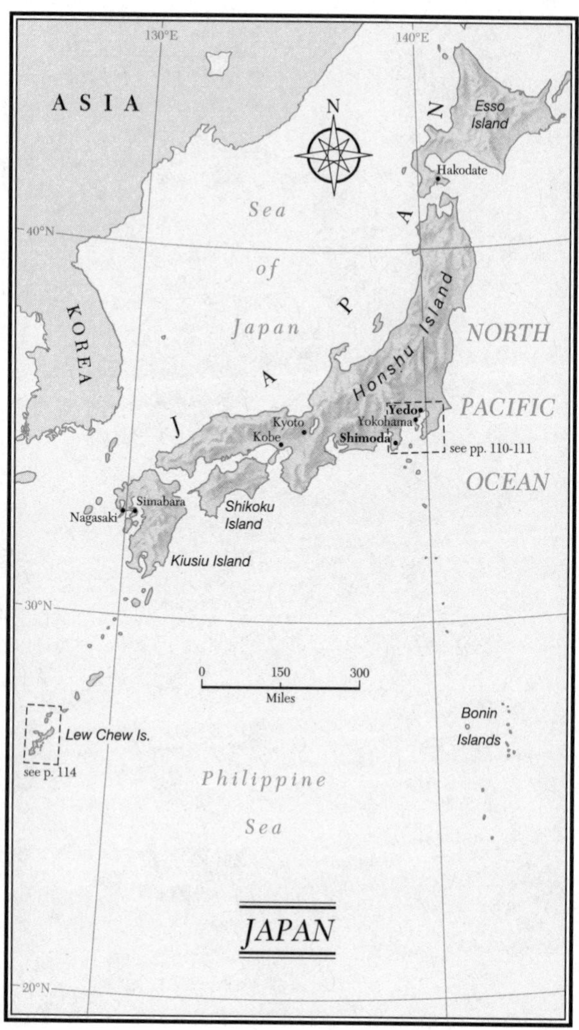
130°E
140°E
ASIA
N
Esso
Island
Hakodate
Sea
of
Japan
40°N
KOREA
J A P A N
Honshu Island
NORTH
PACIFIC
OCEAN
Yedo
Yokohama
Shimoda
Kyoto
Kobe
see pp. 110-111
Simabara
Nagasaki
Shikoku
Island
Kiusiu Island
30°N
0
150
300
Miles
Bonin
Islands
Lew Chew Is.
see p. 114
Philippine
Sea
JAPAN
20°N

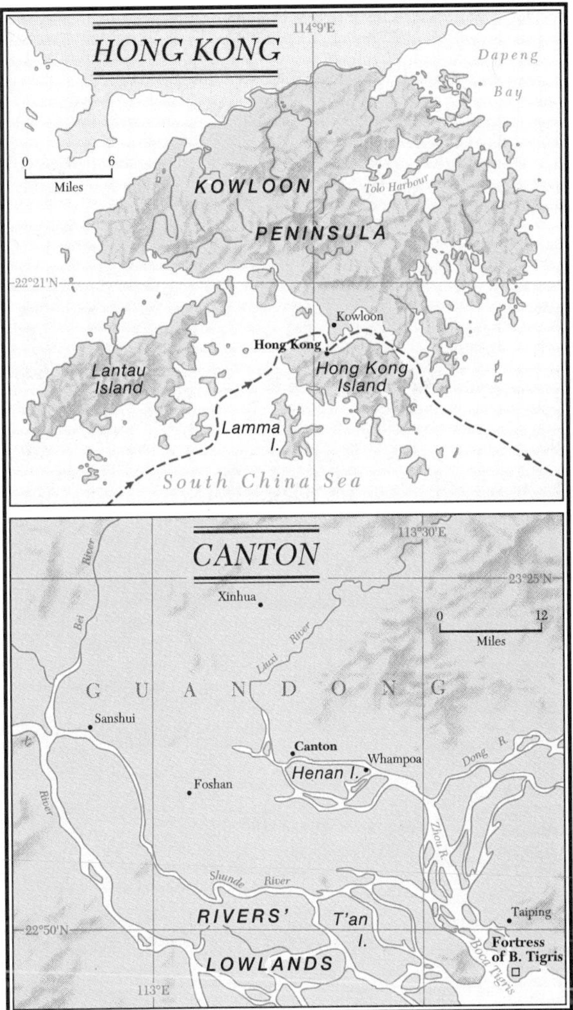
HONG KONG
114°9'E
Dapeng
Bay
0
6
Miles
KOWLOON
PENINSULA
Tolo Harbour
22°21'N
Kowloon
Hong Kong
Hong Kong
Island
Lantau
Island
Lamma
I.
South China Sea
CANTON
113°30'E
23°25'N
Xinhua
0
12
Miles
Bei
River
Liuxi
River
G U A N D O N G
Sanshui
Canton
Whampoa
Henan I.
Dong R.
Foshan
River
Zhou R.
Shunde
River
RIVERS'
T'an
I.
Taiping
22°50'N
Fortress
of B. Tigris
Boca Tigris
LOWLANDS
113°E

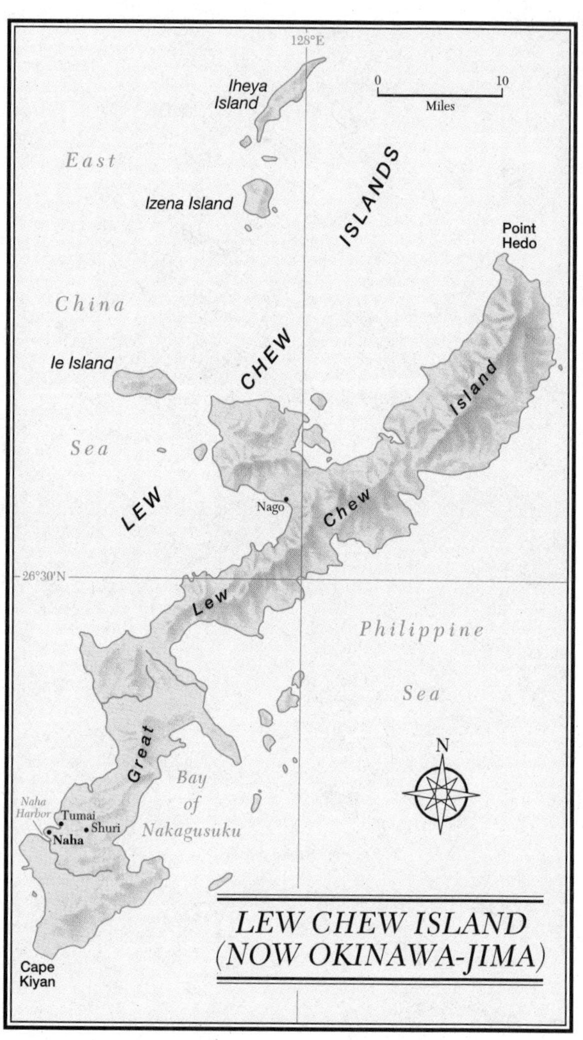
128°E
0
10
Miles
Iheya Island
East
Izena Island
ISLANDS
Point Hedo
China
CHEW
Ie Island
Island
Sea
LEW
Nago
Chew
26°30'N
Lew
Philippine
Sea
Great
N
Bay of Nakagusuku
Naha Harbor
Tumai
Shuri
Naha
Cape Kiyan
LEW CHEW ISLAND (NOW OKINAWA-JIMA)

American sailors hunting wild game with "thunder-tubes"; from the Black Ship Scroll

Perry's men measuring tides, an activity conducted during harbor surveys; from the Black Ship Scroll

Courtesy Honolulu Academy of Arts

Commodore Perry, as perceived and drawn by a Japanese artist, from the Black Ship Scroll

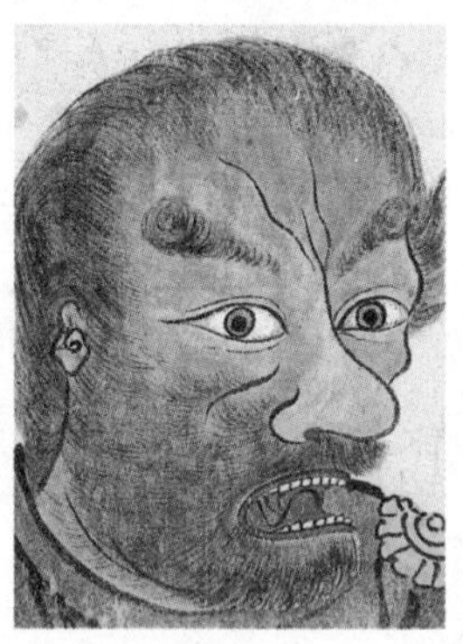

Captain Henry A. Adams, second in command; from the Black Ship Scroll

Courtesy Honolulu Academy of Arts

GUIDE TO PLACE NAMES

Mid Nineteenth Century	*Late Twentieth Century*
CHINA	
Amoy	*Xiamen*
Boca Tigris	*Zhou Jiang*
Canton	*Guangzhou*
Hainan Island	*Hainan Dao [Gaalong Bay, Taya Islands, and Tinhosa Island lie in vicinity of Hainan Island]*
Hankow	*Hankou*
Hoang-Ho River [Yellow River]	*Huang He Jiang*
Hong Kong	*Hong Kong*
Hwangpu River	*Hwiangpu Jiang*
Kiaochow Bay	*[Adjacent to Qingdao]*
Ladrones Islands	*[Lie off the Canton or Pearl (Zhou) River]*
Lymoon Pass	*Lei Mun*
Min River	*Min Jiang*
Nanking	*Nanjing*
Ningpo	*Ningbo*
Peking	*Beijing*
Sancian [or Sanchuen] Island	*[Among Ladrones Islands]*
Shantung Peninsula	*Shandong Bandao*
She-poo	*[Harbor south of Chu-san]*
Swatow	*Shantou*
Tientsin	*Tianjin*
Tsingtao	*Qingdao*
Whampoa	*Huang-pu*
Wusung River	*Wusong or Su Zhou*
Yang-tse [Keang] River	*Chang Jiang*

MID NINETEENTH CENTURY	*LATE TWENTIETH CENTURY*
JAPAN	
Bay of Edo	*Tokyo Bay*
Bungo	*Bungo-suido*
Dezima Island	*Deshima-jima*
Edo [or Yeddo]	*Tokyo*
Esso-jima [or Yesso]	*Hokkaido Island*
Fusiyama	*Mt. Fujiyama*
Hakodate/Hakodadi	*Hakodate*
Honshu-jima	*Honshu Island*
Hyogo	*Kobe*
Kanagawa/Yokohama	*Yokohama*
Kurihama/Gorahama	*Kurihama*
Kyiusiu Island	*Kyushu-jima*
Simoda	*Shimoda*
RYUKYU ISLANDS	
Lew Chew Islands (Liu Ch'iu Islands)	*Ryukyu Islands [Japan]*
Great Lew Chew Island	*Okinawa-jima*
Napa/Napha	*Naha*
Shuri/Shui	*Shuri*
OTHER	
Formosa	*Taiwan*
Gulf of Tonquin	*Gulf of Tonkin [Vietnam]*
Kelung [Formosa]	*Keelung [Taiwan]*
Kokiensan Island	*[Among Majicosimas Islands]*
Madjicosima Islands	*[Lie northeast of Taiwan]*
Ogasawara-gunto	*Bonin Islands [Japan]*
Patchungsan	*[Among Majicosimas Islands]*
Pescadores Islands	*P'enghu Liehtao*

Bibliography of Gazetteers

Chambers World Gazetteer, 5th ed. (Cambridge, UK: Chambers, 1988).

The Columbia Lippincott Gazetteer of the World (New York: Columbia University Press, 1962).

Longman's Gazetteer of the World (London: Longman's Green, 1895).

The Times Index-Gazetteer of the World (London: The Times Publishing Co., 1965).

Webster's New Geographical Dictionary (Springfield, MA: Merriam-Webster, 1984).

slowly wafted in toward the land. Here a new enemy awaited them. Surrounded by trading junks and fishing craft, whose crews would often come on board and lend a hand at the pumps, their crippled condition was speedily recognized. At sundown one afternoon, two piratical luggers laid her alongside and poured a swarm of Celestial cutthroats on board. The captain and mate dashed into the cabin for their firearms; but before a shot could be fired two hundred pirates had overpowered the crew and lashed them to the deck. The captain and mate fought from the cabin as long as their ammunition lasted and then did their best to blow up the ship. Exhausted from loss of blood, they were at last driven from their refuge and bound with the rest of the crew. The pirates looted their prize of everything the typhoon had spared and then vanished in the darkness.

Sometimes these amiable enterprises are conducted by amateurs, so to speak, by your own crew for example, if you happen to have shipped a gang of Chinamen. Things have changed somewhat even in the Central Flowery Kingdom, but time was when a little professional venture of this sort was not uncongenial to the average Chinese coolie, whether ashore or afloat. In 1828 a French merchantman, the *Navigateur,* was wrecked on the coast of Cochin China.* The commander hired a

*Cochin China, the historic designation for southern Vietnam; Saigon was its capital and chief city.–Ed.

junk to carry the remnants of his crew and cargo northward to Macao. As they neared their destination, the natives, five times their number, rose up, murdered all but one, and then made off with booty. That one, after fighting desperately for his life, leaped overboard and was picked up by a passing fisherman. It helps to bear the outrage to know that by his evidence in court, other miscreants were identified and paid for their crime.

There have been bloody epochs in the history of Chinese commerce when piracy was as much an organized system as the opium traffic is now. Whole fleets of sea-robbers prowled about the coasts, plundered villages, levied blackmail on native and foreigner alike, and generally silenced their victims by sending them to the bottom of the sea. Let us not be unreasonable. Those were days of the iron hand everywhere.

Why not give the Mongol his chance as well as the Roman, the Norseman, the Corsican, the Turk? Why not allow the Koshinga to play his drama along with Morgan, Hastings, Kidd, Lafitte, Duval, and all the other great actors of tragedy?*

*Sewall tabs these "iron hand" figures as pirates, which some, though not all, indeed were. Thus: Koshinga from Kwoshinga, widely known as Kosinga (1624–62), a fervent Ming loyalist against the Ch'ing (Manchu) conquest of China; possibly Sir Henry Morgan (1635–88), a British buccaneer; possibly Warren Hastings (1732–1818), a highly controversial administrator of India; William Kidd (1645?–1701), a Scottish pirate; Jean LaFitte (ca. 1780–ca. 1826), a pirate; Claude Duval (1643–70), a noted highwayman in England.–Ed.

Chinese annals record two periods during which these marauding fleets became so powerful and insolent that the empire with all its resources could not yet destroy them nor even repel their attacks. There is plenty of romance in the story.

The most famous corsairs known to Chinese history, most famous perhaps because of their ferociousness, were a father and son, Ching Chelung and Ching Chingkung.

They flourished about the time of the Manchu conquest in 1644. The son was familiarly called Kwoshing, but is better known by his Portuguese Latinized name Koshinga. The father, after years of adventure, honest and dishonest, untold and untellable, found himself at the head of an immense nondescript fleet with which he harried the helpless coasts and laid waste the seas. Bribes of wealth and rank decoyed the redoubtable chieftain into the imperial service. He was made supreme commander of the Chinese navy. In his new position it became his duty to protect commerce and destroy piracy. He accordingly protected commerce and destroyed piracy. He knew how. No petty scruples of honor or generous memory stood in the way. It was as a sort of grim atonement for his own crimes that whole squadrons of his former comrades were, with unpitying impartiality, dispatched to their infernal shades.

He assumed the monopoly of all lucrative commerce and levied tribute on all manner of craft. He did what he liked, and no power in the empire dared question his right. The emperor even bestowed on his son in marriage a princess of the blood. In course of time his unchallenged supremacy made him careless. Detected in an intrigue against the government he was enticed to court and there found himself in a gilded cage beyond whose bars he was never again permitted to go. There he languished for many years where he finally died as a prisoner of state.

It would take lurid colors to paint the wrath of Koshinga when it became apparent that the old tiger, his sire, was held in hopeless captivity. No doubt the atmosphere reeked with Chinese rhetoric. Vowing eternal hate to the whole Tatar race, he summoned his fellow ruffians and betook himself to this home on the wave. This was in 1646. For more than thirty years his name was the terror of the seas. He preyed upon commerce until from sheer fright, commerce shut itself up in port and dared not come out. As a result the few prizes he caught were not enough to maintain and feed his vast squadron. Then he invaded the shores and plundered not only villages and towns but capital cities and provinces. He besieged Nanking. He captured and fortified Amoy. He finally stole and occupied the island of Formosa, seized the government, established arsenals and ports for his fleets, and thence hurled his filibustering raids upon the opposite coasts.

At last his bloody incursions became such an intolerable scourge to the empire, which could neither prevent nor resist them, that the extraordinary measure was adopted of abandoning for the time all trade on the seas and withdrawing the entire population from the coast. This was actually done, probably the only instance of its kind in history, and the Chinese were the only people who would ever have dreamed of tactics so absurd and so masterly. For hundreds of leagues up and down the shores of the great realm there stretched between the hungry vampires and their victims a strip of abandoned seacoast twelve miles broad, whose fields lay untilled, whose once populous cities and villages lay deserted and crumbling in decay, whose useless junks slumbered and foundered at their moorings in the harbors. Byron's "dream which was not all a dream" sounds almost like the work of a newspaper reporter writing up the details:

> "The rivers, lakes and ocean all stood still,
> And nothing stirred within their silent depths,
> Ships sailorless, lay rotting on the sea."

Macao was excepted, and that because the Portuguese colonists were presumed to be competent to protect themselves. It was seven years before the deserted sea-fringe of the empire was reoccupied and trade was allowed to flow into its wonted channels. The death of the dreaded Koshinga soon after closed the seventeenth-century piratical era.

Minor adventurers still carried on their more stealthy depredations, and have done so intermittently ever since. The growing value of an increasing commerce, along with the addition of several priceless argosies from Europe and from America, furnished ample temptation.

In December 1806, the mate of an English ship was captured and brought into the presence of the commandant of the fleet. He found himself in a squadron of some six hundred junks and lorchas, carrying batteries of from six to eighteen pounders, and classed in five divisions under five independent chiefs. During his captivity he became familiar with the entire system, its organization, its stringent regulations, the numbers and armament of the divisions, their plans and methods of attack. After some five months of captivity, he was finally ransomed. Three years later another Englishman fell into their hands. The fleet had grown. There were six divisions. The total force operating, though rarely all together, he estimated at eight hundred large vessels and a thousand smaller craft, carrying a complement of some seventy thousand men. The atrocities he witnessed are detailed with a sailor's frankness and do not make pleasant reading. It was the destruction wreaked by Koshinga *redivivus*, only this time it was worse.

The Englishman's story fully corroborates the chronicle written down by Yung-lun-yuen, a Chinese scholar who was a contemporary of the bloody actors and exploits he describes. The six squadrons sailed under six flags—red, yellow, black, blue, green, and white. It was the yellow fleet that has furnished this chapter with its label, for it was the admiral of the yellow, Woo-che-tsing, who assumed the winsome title "Scourge of the Eastern Seas." If actions speak louder than words, he more than made his title good. The red fleet is of still more thrilling interest, partly because it outnumbered all the rest put together, partly because it was for a time commanded by a woman. In 1807 the arch-outlaw Ching-yih, who had driven it into the smoke and flame of many a desperate conflict, perished in a violent storm. His widow at once took command, and in a hundred fights, demonstrated that she had inherited the temper and prowess of her bloody mate. The "new woman" had come. Men feared and obeyed. She maintained the discipline of a martinet and exacted implicit submission. Never was petticoat government more strenuous or more efficient. She was punctilious in her dealings with the folk on shore and, by honest and liberal payment for supplies, won their confidence and favor—a policy the other divisions of the fleet might have followed with advantage.

Some of the exploits of these red-rovers are curiously interesting. If any of my readers have sailed up the Canton River, you will recall the Chinese fortress of the Boca Tigris at its mouth, on the starboard side as you enter. Down by the waterside a long white parapet stretches along the shore; at each end a wall reaches up the hill and disappears over the crest. Whether there is a fourth wall out of sight, joining the two and completing the square, I do not remember; but certain British tars could tell you if they have lasted from 1841 to this present year of grace. During the Opium War the fortress was attacked.* The storming party pulled quietly around the headland and, forming on the beach, clambered up over the hill; the first notice the Celestials had that they were being attacked was the sight of the foreign troops rushing down upon them from the rear within the walls. There was nothing for it but to surrender. They surrendered, therefore, but bristling with wrath at such a breach of military manners. "Hiyah! Why you no come front side! More better make fight where we make ready!"

It was an earlier commandant of this same fortress who met with equally bad luck. One of the fleets appeared in his neighborhood, and he sallied out to attack it. The pirates surrounded him, and after a furious action that lasted all day and with such havoc as may better be left to the imagination, captured him and such fragments of his fleet as were still afloat. This disaster was partly avenged

*The three Opium Wars (1839–42, 1858, and 1859) forced upon China the system of so-called unequal treaties, which opened ports to commerce and included the humiliation of extraterritorial privileges for foreigners, Americans among them, of immunity from local law enforcement.—Ed.

the next year when the Chinese admiral with a hundred junks attacked another fleet on the same cruising ground. Great numbers of the pirates were destroyed and some two hundred taken prisoner. If you are familiar with Chinese methods, you can readily judge how long the two hundred were kept from joining their bloody shipmates in the shades below. In another encounter not far from the same place, before the combatants could close upon one another, it fell dead calm, whereupon crowds of the pirates leaped into the sea like savages, swam to the enemy with their knives in their teeth, and attacked with such fierceness that they could not be beaten off, and actually cut out several junks from the imperial fleet. The fortunes of war varied. With provoking impartiality and apparently showing no preference on the score of justice or ethics, victory would perch on the standard of the pirate as often as on the banners of the righteous defenders of their country. We read of whole squadrons engaged, fighting all day and all night, two days, even three days at a time, two hundred or three hundred junks on a side, and a drawn game at the end. No child's play this. At one time the admiral was lying quietly at anchor among the islands; suddenly two hundred pirate craft slip around the headland and pounce upon him with an onset so furious that twenty-five of his fleet are gone with their captors before he can get up his anchors and chase them.

These conflicts were not confined only to the sea.

There were raids on the villages that lined the harbors and rivers. Spies made their way into the bazaars disguised as peddlers, barbers, traders; if they came out alive they brought news to the waiting fleet where were to be found the easiest conquests and the richest booty. Sometimes the villagers fled, and the women and cattle were scooped up by the invaders; sometimes they made a stand, and the bloody struggle proved the valor of the longshoreman as well as of the bandit. Large towns were sacked, and prisoners were gathered not by the score only or by the hundred but even by the thousand. Some unique exploits are recorded. When Mei-ying, the bonny wife of Kee-chu-yang, was captured, she railed at her captors with such stinging eloquence that one of the ruffians knocked her down; whereupon she leaped to her feet, seized him with her teeth, and sprang overboard, dragging the brute with her to a watery grave.

It more than once happened that when a commander found the brigands were too many for him and were closing in upon him for the *coup de grâce*, he retreated to the magazine and turned the tables on them by blowing himself and them out of the water. On one occasion, by a stroke of fortune, the pirate fleet was caught and penned in its own lair. Great preparations were made for a mighty stroke of destruction. Twenty-five fire junks were sent blazing in among the anchored craft. The imperial fleet followed, intending by a supreme blow to annihilate the whole bloody horde. With the corsairs it was a fight for life. Anyone who has witnessed a Chinese battle can imagine the uproar of such an encounter. Hundreds of the pirates paid the penalty of their crimes, but the mangled remnant of their fleet broke through the blockade and scuttled out to the open sea. The plucky admiral pursued them and sank a few more. After dark, they turned back on him and repaid him in kind.

Among such turbulent spirits, we need not wonder if the internal conditions were not always serene. In process of time, a violent feud broke out in the squadron under the petticoat chief. Words came to blows. The mutineers drew off their clientele and staked their destiny on a pitched battle. The vanquished party after an overwhelming defeat concluded to retire from business and submit to government. We get an inkling of the magnitude of these operations from the fact that this one capitulation included no less than some eight thousand men, about 126 vessels, some five hundred battery guns, and several thousand stand of miscellaneous arms.[2] The commander of the defunct fleet was honored with a government position.

This appealed to the heart of the widow chieftain. Perhaps a life spent among scenes of carnage may have begun to pall upon her. She negotiated. And, after various diplomatic interchanges, assured at last of safety, she decided to capitulate, and, with

[2]Yung-Jun-yuen, 74–75.

the wives and children of some of her officers, the bloodstained tigress presented herself before the governor general at Canton. The pardon accorded by government put an end to what was left of the famous red squadron and cleaned out the middle and eastern channels of the Canton River. Many of her red-handed followers enlisted in the imperial fleets and were put at once to the work of "pacification." The other fleets were destroyed or saved themselves by submission. The "Scourge of the Eastern Seas" came in with the rest and so retained his worthless head. And the Chinese historian who is my authority for this *dénouement* adds with a cheerful optimism that is hardly sustained by the sequel, that now, (that is, in 1810) "ships pass and repass in tranquillity. All is quiet on the rivers, the four seas are tranquil, and people live in peace and plenty."

But an opulent commerce, growing richer every year, was very attractive and made piracy as tempting as ever. And so it came to pass that the great "pacification" of 1810 did not stay pacified. The China seas have never since been vexed by such enormous squadrons of buccaneers, nor have witnessed such tremendous battles; but local adventurers have been plentiful and, on occasion, have combined into very considerable fleets. The Chinese navy has now and then roused itself to a spurt of zeal, but has never accomplished much in the way of clearing the seas; apparently it has not had much stomach for the attempt. Most of the actual suppression of Chinese piracy has been due to the courage and skill of British tars.

Many officers of the Royal Navy, while serving in the East, have had a hand in the exciting task of ferreting out and destroying these highwaymen of the sea. Captain St. John, who was thus employed for several years, gives graphic details of his various expeditions, now chasing them into the winding channels that form so large a part of the intricate network of the Canton River, now surprising them in the snug harbors where they lay concealed behind the hills. His account of their attack on the mail steamer plying between Hong Kong and Canton gives a sample of their audacity. A fleet of forty-four junks pounced upon her from the reaches that open into the river; she had to run the gauntlet of them all and was badly hulled with shot before she managed to escape.

On another page he describes a large opium junk that lay at anchor close by his own berth. She was bound up the coast to Swatow, and with a crew of forty-five and a full battery of twelve and eighteen pounders seemed so absolutely secure that some forty passengers came on board to take advantage of a conveyance so safe. She got underway at nightfall but had scarcely cleared the Lymoon Pass before it fell calm and she was obliged to anchor. At midnight a large junk slipped quietly alongside, boarded her, and overpowered the watch on deck before they fairly knew they were attacked. The passengers and crew were driven below and secured under hatches and the vessel taken around to a secluded spot on the south side of the island, where every soul on board except a small boy was lashed hand and foot and flung overboard. The junk was then rifled and sunk.

It is an immense satisfaction to know that these miscreants occasionally fall into their own traps. The fate they prepare for their victims rebounds, and they get a taste of their own villainy. A thrilling adventure of this sort happened to Major Shore of the English army. Having occasion just after the Opium War to visit Ningpo, he was obliged to return at once and at night over a route swarming with pirates. He was in a Chinese passage boat, his own little boy the only other passenger, and his only weapons two double-barreled duck guns and a brace of heavy pistols. The night was still and he slept with his guns for company. Just before daybreak one of his boatmen, blanched with terror, roused him with the news that the pirates were coming. He seized his arms and leaped on deck. The silvery mist of the dawn obscured his vision, but presently he made out a dark object looming through the haze, a large and ugly-looking boat crowded with a gang of assassins stealthily creeping toward his defenseless craft. One can imagine his reflections in the brief interval before they would be alongside. His only chance lay in giving them such a sudden and hot reception that they would suppose his boat filled with men. He could see them now, a score of bronze villains with long knives in their hands, some of them stripped to the waist, some of them with dirks stuck through the coils of their pigtails. There they crouched like tigers ready to spring, as vicious a lot as ever murdered an honest crew. For just such game as this, if he should have the ill fortune to meet any, he had taken the safe precaution to load each barrel with a double charge, and, as it would not do to misfire, he reprimed his percussion locks with fresh caps. In the deathly stillness he even noticed the ticking of his watch and the beating of his heart, and "wondered how soon both would cease forever."

Crouching behind the rail and scarcely breathing until the boats were within ten yards of each other, he took careful aim and then let drive both barrels straight in the ruffians' faces. Shrieks of rage and pain and a crash of tumbling bodies bore witness to the execution. Those two shots cleared the forecastle. Not daring to lose any chances, he seized the other gun and blazed away at the crowd in the waist. Another yell, a panic, and a babel of confusion. He was swiftly reloading when a ball from a swivel gun on the pirates' bow whizzed by his head and shivered the mast. The savage who had thus missed his mark was apparently the leader of the gang, a muscular chief whose giant frame loomed dark against the gray dawn. Then the major instantly covered him with a pistol; a sharp explosion, and the miscreant with his fuse still burning pitched headlong into the black waters beneath.

At this final blow the pirates stood not on the order of their going but incontinently fled. The passage boat with sail and oars scuttled away from so dangerous a neighborhood at the top of her speed. The chastisement inflicted by the brave major taught the brigands a lesson not soon forgotten. It was a long time before they dared attack anything, native or foreign, until well assured that their victim was unarmed, or that they could dash upon him unawares.

While the southern coast seems to have been the favorite field of operation for these Celestial vikings, the northern seas have also suffered from the same dread scourge. None of the estuaries of the north are so admirably contrived for buccaneering purposes as the Canton River, with its countless branches, channels, and creeks; but there are plenty of islands and jutting capes and snug coves behind or within which any discreet pirate could conduct his business in safe seclusion. Whoever, therefore, has had the occasion to entrust himself to wind and wave on errands of commerce or science or travel has found it to his advantage to take account of the corsairs as one of the perils of the deep.

Mr. Fortune describes in his entertaining book a trip he once took on the steamer *Erin* from Ningpo to Shanghai. They had scarcely cleared the river

Min below the city when they found themselves in the midst of a squadron of freebooters engaged in blockading the passage between Silver Island and the shore and capturing every sort of native craft that attempted to run the gauntlet in or out. Some of the prizes were plundered at once and turned adrift. The more valuable were taken to the pirates' den to be held until ransomed by their rich owners in Ningpo. Negotiations would be carried on sometimes for weeks and all the while a posse of Chinese men-of-war sleeping lazily at their anchors within half a dozen miles of the scene. The *Erin* threaded her way through the fleet unmolested, witnessing as she passed the capture of a big Shantung junk they had decoyed into their ambuscade. "During the time they were in sight," Mr. Fortune continues, "we observed several vessels from the north fall into their hands. They were in such numbers and their plans were so well laid that nothing that passed in daylight could possibly escape. Long after we had lost sight of their vessels we saw and pitied the unsuspecting northern junks running down with a fair wind and all sail into the trap which had been prepared for them."

In a short time, however, the avenging furies were on the track of the outlaws. On her way up the coast, the *Erin* met an English cruiser, which was called *Bittern*, and gave her the needed information. The rendezvous of the piratical fleet was found to be at She-poo, a landlocked harbor a few miles south of Chusan. The *Bittern* headed for She-poo with her ally the *Paoushan*, a steamer that had been recently purchased and equipped by a company of Chinese merchants for the protection of their commerce. The pirates had a well-organized system of sentries and spies and knew of their assailants long before they appeared off the narrow entrance to the harbor. Confident in their overwhelming numbers they welcomed the two vessels with derisive yells and the deafening clamor of guns and gongs.

The steamer towed the brig into position, where she leisurely anchored, so close to the pirate lines that the storm of shot from their batteries passed over her and splashed harmlessly into the water beyond. Her response was something terrific. The first broadside demolished or sank more than one of the braggart junks. Her guns were aimed by British gunners and every shot told. Junk after junk went to the bottom. The derisive yells were turned into shrieks of terror and pain. The harbor was strewn with mangled wreckage and floating bodies. Hundreds of the pirates were mowed down by shot and shell or were drowned as they dashed overboard and vainly struck out for land. Some two hundred or three hundred succeeded in scrambling on shore and, by throwing up a hasty redoubt, mounted some guns. A squad of British tars landed in pursuit and, by a swift flank movement, routed them to the four winds. The victory was supreme. The annihilation of the pirates and their fleet was as great a surprise and almost as complete as though a volcano had suddenly risen in their midst with a fiery eruption in full blast. The throngs of village and country folk who crowded the hillsides around the bay were lost in admiration at the bravery of the "foreign devils." How the plucky little brig and her consort dared venture into the tiger's dangerous lair and grapple such an enormously superior force was a miracle quite beyond the Celestial imagination.

But the centuries pass. Even China yields to the pressure of modern life. Railroads are beginning to run their lines of steel toward the heart of the empire. Telegraphs and telephones are spinning their web of wires over all the land. The government is minting its own coinage, developing its mines with Yankee machinery, establishing arsenals, steam-works, navy yards like the rest of the world. Chinese schools are teaching science developed in the West. Christian missions are disseminating a higher faith, a purer morality, and a more rational civilization. The same progressive spirit has laid hold of commerce. The sleepy junk cannot keep pace with the swift demands of business. Now along the vast waterfront of fifteen hundred miles, most of the carrying trade is handled by a fleet of jaunty steamers owned by the government and sailed by European officers. The inland waters are open to steam navigation, foreign as well as native, and that means not only an enormous increase of commerce but also the penetration of the Chinese world in every direction with Western ideas. It may indeed happen that an occasional paroxysm of reaction, like the Boxer massacres, may sweep over some section of the great empire and may for the time turn all progress and all hope into chaos. But the world moves fast. And no oriental barrier can long withstand the flood tide of modern civilization.

These forward movements are enough to make old Koshinga's bones rattle in his tomb. The modern bandit, too, looks out from his lair with consternation. His old lorchas and Mandarin boats are no match for steam. He can do little more than a small and stealthy retail business. A sudden dash upon a lonely trader and a stab in the dark may win an occasional prize; but let him come out into the open and dare anything on a larger scale, and the imperial steam navy would speedily hunt him down on his own blood-stained seas. And if the Yellow Dragon needs help in the operation, many another knight errant like Chinese Gordon would be eager to volunteer.*

*For Chinese Gordon in the Taiping Rebellion, see Chapter VIII.–Ed.

VI

Bound for the Sunrise Kingdom

JAPAN IS the Emerald Isle of the East. Its people call it the Empire of the Rising Sun. Its sun is rising fast. The transformation is so complete that the Japan of fifty years ago is forever past and gone. When I dream over again the adventures of that famous expedition, I seem to be sitting among the shadows of past centuries and watching the argosies of the middle ages or the buccaneering voyages of Raleigh and Cavendish and Drake.*

In the summer of 1872 Mr. Mori, then the Japanese minister at Washington, made a speech in English before an educational convention in Boston. I could hardly credit my senses as I listened and thought of the marvelous change. Only nineteen years before I had witnessed the strange scenes which befell on those mysterious shores, where by the laws of the realm it was death for a foreigner to set his foot; and here already was an educated Japanese gentleman habited in Western costume and

*Sir Walter Raleigh (1552–1618), English soldier, courtier, explorer, and man of letters; Sir Thomas Cavendish (1555–92) ravaged the Spanish Main and led three English ships around the world between 1586 and 1588; Sir Francis Drake (1540?–96), navigator and admiral, the first Englishman to circumnavigate the world.–Ed.

addressing us in our own language! It was one of the miracles of history. Other miracles–political, commercial, social, martial–have followed in swift succession. And they have so transformed the Japan of the dark ages into an enlightened modern nation keeping step with the civilization of the West, and now standing in line with the other world powers that one can hardly remember there ever was a blind past of superstition and isolation.

The interest felt in our oriental venture was not confined to America. Over that secluded land on the rim of the world had always brooded a cloud of mystery; and that threw a sort of halo over the fleet itself. Its progress was watched by all of Europe. Japan, too, was on alert, for the air was thick with rumors, and the coming squadron was casting its shadows before. There are reasons, of course, why we Americans should feel a special concern in our own enterprise. As it was American diplomacy that unlocked the gates of the Sunrise Kingdom to the outside world, so American institutions have largely furnished the models for the reconstruction of her social and political life. And by the great highway of the Pacific, America lies nearest to the marts of commerce and trade thus laid open to the fleets of the West.

But why send an expedition to those distant shores? What was our interest in Japan, or Japan's interest in us, that should prompt such a mission? The letter Commodore Perry bore from our gov-

Millard Fillmore

Daniel Webster

Edward Everett

Franklin Pierce

Photos Courtesy National Archives, College Park, Maryland

ernment to the Mikado asked for a mutual treaty.[1] The original instrument was drafted in May 1851, by Daniel Webster, then Secretary of State, and was signed by President Fillmore. There it rested. Perhaps the presidential autograph and seal proved too heavy a dignity. At any rate it never rose after that, and it never got to Japan.

In November 1852, Webster's successor, Edward Everett, fished it out of the departmental pigeonhole, took it to pieces, and re-fashioned it. Three copies were prepared and all were splendidly engrossed in English, Dutch, and in Chinese. These were enclosed together in a sumptuous gold case; and, to make the whole presentment still more impressive to the Japanese mind, the gold case was enshrined in a coffer of rosewood. This was the precious missive borne by the American fleet. One would hardly think so small a package would require a whole squadron to carry it. Why would not

[1]It has greatly interested me to discover that the original suggestion which led to this treaty came from my late neighbor and friend, Hannibal Hamlin, Senator from Maine, afterwards Vice President with Abraham Lincoln. "His attention was drawn to the possibilities of trade which the United States might build up with oriental nations. On February 21, 1850, he introduced a resolution calling on the Secretary of State for whatever information he might possess covering these points [abuse of our sailors, and possibilities of trade] and also requesting him to report on the advisability of appointing a commissioner or diplomatic agent to open up amicable relations and negotiate commercial treaties with these nations." *Life and Times of Hannibal Hamlin*, by his grandson, Charles Eugene Hamlin, p. 230.

a single messenger of peace be more appropriate than batteries and guns? The lords of creation do not commonly make their proposals to the weaker sex at the cannon's mouth. But Japan was a somewhat supercilious dame and had hotly resented such overtures before. She would do so again.

There was no reason to expect that the haughty empire would deign to receive, much less to read and answer, any appeal from the outside barbarian world unless backed by a force capable of making its mission respected. America had reason to demand a hearing, and her fleet made it possible to get it. The document entrusted to Commodore Perry asked of the Japanese court two things, friendship and trade. Friendship, for the safety of our seamen; that first and foremost. Many a hapless crew had been driven into their ports by storm or wrecked on their rocky coast, escaping the perils of the deep only to be welcomed to a dungeon or a cage on shore. This wrong must be stopped at all hazards. And if in addition we could persuade Japan to enter into friendly relations of trade, the two countries by mutual interchange of productions might promote each its own prosperity and the welfare of the other. It was thought that an Oriental might see that as well as a Yankee. In the end they did. It cannot be said that Japan ever really yearned to be "opened" anymore than an oyster does; yet when the time came, she yielded as gracefully as any oyster I ever had the pleasure of meeting.

Commodore Perry's Visit to Shuri, Lew Chew; from The Expedition of an American Squadron

Courtesy The Beverly R. Robinson Collection, United States Naval Academy Museum, Annapolis, Maryland

Commodore Matthew Calbraith Perry reached Hong Kong in the steam frigate *Mississippi* April 7, 1853. His arrival produced the usual flurry of rumors; and when the air cleared, the one fact left that specially concerned us was that the *Saratoga* would be detained to form a part of the great expedition. The appointed term of our cruise was up, indeed, or would be by the time we could reach home. But the squadron was small at best, and the commodore could ill afford to spare a single ship; and on our own part a visit to that mysterious land was too big a thing to miss.

We wasted no time in bewailing our fate. Orders flew thick and fast from the flagship, and a month was spent in miscellaneous preparations, diplomatic, financial, and commissariat. The beginnings of even the famous movements of history are prosaic. At last, all the fleet was safely gathered at the appointed rendezvous, Napa, the chief harbor of Lew Chew. The *Saratoga* brought from Macao the interpreter, Dr. S. Wells Williams; and as we neared the entrance, we met the *Susquehanna* and the *Mississippi* just going in. They had come from Shanghai; some days later, the *Plymouth* appeared from the same quarter. These four, with the storeships *Supply* and *Caprice*, constituted our entire force in the China Seas. A small armada with which to "open" an empire!

It might seem that since the fleet was all present, the one thing to do was to up anchor and make straight for Japan. But expeditions are ponderous things. They do not go off like a rocket. Beside the main issue, there are other matters, more and of larger concern than are dreamed of in common philosophy. And while the commodore and his satraps are attending to these, the rest of us can take to the road and idle about in whatever direction the scenery or the people may promise entertainment. We may not get to Japan in this chapter, but if the functionaries are duly deliberate we may have leisure to observe diverse and sundry things.

The Lew Chew Islands are velveted with a quiet garden-like verdure that gives them an air of peaceful dignity. The interior is more picturesque than the borderline of the shore. The well-groomed valleys are separated from each other sometimes by crags whose ragged heights are festooned with masses of trailing vines, sometimes by smoothly rounded summits where grow side by side with equal ease and no envious rivalry the tropical palm and the northern pine. The natives impressed us as a courteous and sedate folk, somewhat stately and reserved, yet amply endowed with human nature.

A British flag, which was flung to the breeze as we neared the anchorage, marked the residence of the only white man in the group, the missionary Dr. Bettelheim. We found him to be an interesting man. He was sent there by the London Naval Mission; he faithfully worked for the good of the natives. He furnished us with vocabularies; it was not long

Regent of Lew Chew; from The Expedition of an American Squadron

Courtesy The Beverly R. Robinson Collection, United States Naval Academy Museum, Annapolis, Maryland

before we could *parlez-vous* with the people in their own language, at least on such momentous facts as poultry, potatoes, plantains, and pigs. Though just outside the tropics, we found the islands richly embellished with tropical growth to the hilltops; and the transparent waters of the bay revealed gardens of many-hued coral beneath. The diving apparatus was at various times brought into requisition to examine the bottoms of the ships. I remember one afternoon, the diver, having finished his task, took his boat to a submerged reef, threw over his ladder, and descended for a stroll in the coral gardens below. It was like wandering through the pleasure grounds of Neptune's palace, among shrubbery, brilliant with parti-colored flowers and fruit. Coming to the edge of the reef, he threw over his ladder again and, climbing downward, came presently to a cave in the cliff, which he entered and explored. Perhaps he was prospecting for "full many a gem," which the poet declares "the dark unfathomed caves of ocean bear." One cannot help wondering how the poet knew. Had he been a diver? But all the gems our submarine prospector found were alive and wonderfully chromatic and tame; children of the sea of fairy shape and rainbow colors that were flitting in and out or gathering in respectful shoals around him and watching with eager curiosity the movements of this *lusus naturae*, which had invaded their watery realm. They scarcely protested when he even took them in his hands to examine their very graceful shape and their iridescent scales.

While we lay at anchor, two episodes lent a mild flavor of interest to the passing days. One was an official visit of the commodore with a big retinue to Shuri, the capital of Lew Chew, where they were fraternally entertained by the regent, his staff, and crowds of curious spectators, who in turn were themselves immensely entertained by the band music, the gilt trimmings of their foreign guests, and the general outlandishness of the pageant. The other was an exploring party sent out to examine the geology of the island, its agricultural conditions, the people and their modes of life. Bayard Taylor* was a member of this reconnoitering squad and, on its return, wrote out the official report. This was the first introduction of most of us to the young traveler. He was not yet twenty-nine but had already acquired distinction both as a traveler and as a writer. His stalwart manhood impressed us. There was a genial look on his face that reflected a generous nature within; yet there were lines that had been traced by suffering; and we learned afterwards of the death of his young wife two years before. On his way home from Egypt and the Soudan he had been turned back by an order from the New York *Tribune* directing him to meet the expedition in China and accompany it to Japan. He overtook

*Bayard Taylor (1825–78), an American journalist and author of travel books, novels, and poetry. Appointed United States Minister to Germany in 1878, he died in Berlin.–Ed.

Chief Magistrate of Naha, Lew Chew; from The Expedition of an American Squadron

Courtesy University of Chicago Library

the commodore at Shanghai and found, to his surprise, that for an outsider to get a chance in the navy, especially for such an unusual mission, required not only diplomacy and red tape but a large amount of persistence. Finally, the commodore consented, and the young aspirant, destined afterwards to be a foreign ambassador himself, was duly rated on the ship's muster-roll as a master's mate—a dignity about corresponding to the rank of passed midshipman. He was not the only man who coveted a place in the expedition. Many of the gentlemen occupying commercial and official positions in Chinese ports were intensely interested, and several of them made earnest endeavors to capture a berth in it. I remember a resident of Hong Kong sent me a fervent request for the use of my clerkship for a few weeks, even to the extent of offering a year's salary for the privilege. Bayard Taylor adorned the modest rank of master's mate for some four months and, with the commodore, visited Lew Chew and the Bonins before starting for Japan. In both the commodore sent out exploring parties to make a study of the islands and their resources.

Bayard Taylor was a member of both missions. He wrote out the official report of the first, and must have had a hand in the other also as he was the leader of one of the two divisions. His diary of experiences in this naval service must have been entertaining, but alas it is buried fathoms deep in the naval archives at Washington. In accordance with an order issued by the commodore to all who kept journals of the expedition, he turned it in to the Navy department and never saw it again.[2] When the squadron came away from the first visit to Japan, he laid down his mateship and returned to New York in December of that year.

On the ninth of June, leaving two or three of her consorts at anchor, the *Susquehanna* got under way with the *Saratoga* in tow and left the harbor on a tour of observation. Very nice and comfortable to be tied to the apron strings of a motherly steam frigate when you want to get somewhere and the wind is either dead calm or dead ahead. Our objective was the Bonin Islands or, as on Japanese charts, the Ogasawara, a group some eight hundred miles to the eastward of Lew Chew. The commodore was in quest of a coaling station for future transpacific lines of ocean greyhounds. Nobody dreamed then that the Philippines and that Guam would sometime drop into our lap. And commodores being no more omniscient than the rest of us, such a surprise could not be foreseen; otherwise he would have had no interest in the Bonins, and we should have missed a unique experience.

In due time the islands began to lift in dim tracery on the eastern horizon; a rugged group of volcanic fragments upheaved from the floor of the

[2]His impressions of the Sunrise Kingdom and of the famous embassy were embodied a year or two later in a volume entitled *A Visit to India, China and Japan in the Year 1853.*

Natural Tunnel, Port Lloyd, Bonin Islands; from
The Expedition of an American Squadron

Courtesy University of Chicago Library

ocean in some dire geologic convulsion ages ago; serving in recent times for the occupancy of wild hogs and goats and a score of human waifs almost as wild who had drifted thither from sundry corners of the earth. The harbor in which we came to anchor, Port Lloyd, is said to be the submerged crater of an ancient volcano whose hot fires were long since extinguished by the sea. One can well believe it when he finds his anchorage in some eighteen to twenty-two fathoms;* he shuffles off a mortal coil of cable and before it stops running out, his anchor seems to be going down into the Earth's very bowels.

Here, as at Lew Chew, exploring parties prowled through the interior and found it more mountainous, more tangled, and more picturesque than Lew Chew. The heights were crowned to their craggy tops with trees of great variety and often of brilliant beauty. From the summit one could trace the irregular shores of the three main islands, Stapleton, Peel, and Buckland, and could count the brood of callow islets and rocks that littered the sea around them. There was plenty of occupation for the four days we lay at Port Lloyd; climbing the hills, threading the forest, visiting the inhabitants, pulling about the harbor, exploring the cave in the cliff at the entrance. You could pull in through the arch by boat; inside, an enormous cavern big enough to hold the ship. We landed on the beach within and, up on its topside, as a Chinaman would express it,

*One fathom equals six feet.—Ed.

saw another opening through which we crawled and found ourselves facing the ocean outside. I remember digging from a seam in the cliff close by a tolerable specimen of opal. The seine netted us bushels of delicious mullet, and trips to the reefs outside brought in *chelonia* enough to make turtle soup for the whole ship's company for weeks. Some of these immense armor-plated beasts were four, five, even six feet long. Two or three of them we carried to sea with us, and when the men were holystoning the decks in the early morning it was a favorite amusement with them to trot out the turtles and have a ride or rather a crawl on their backs. They were automobiles but not of the racing kind.

The hook and line brought us only fisherman's luck. One calm lazy afternoon the first lieutenant proposed a fishing party outside. The captain's gig was borrowed for the occasion, and into the stern sheets he stowed himself, the doctor, the master, and, by a streak of good luck, the clerk. In a very few minutes our boat's crew put us on our fishing ground and there we lavished the various seductive arts known to the craft. In vain; only one solitary fish could we persuade to leave the briny deep and come in out of the wet, but that one was so gorgeously caparisoned he must have been a member of the royal family. We were fishing in some eight or ten fathoms. Looking over the side we could clearly see bottom through the liquid azure and not merely the bottom, but a submarine rose garden of coral and shoals of little finny cupids playing to and fro in the watery bowers as brilliant as the coral—a kind of living symphony of color. My fish appeared to be about the size of my finger when he cautiously essayed a lunch off my hook and then started so suddenly for the upper regions; but when he came sailing in over the thwarts, he was twelve or fifteen inches long, and from stem to stern one glowing splendor of scarlet more brilliant than any goldfish I ever saw. We held a naval court martial over our trophy and sent him on board the flagship to sit for his portrait with Mr. Heine, the artist of the expedition. And when afterwards the Congressional Report of the Japan expedition came out, there was my fish, not so resplendent as in life, but a very fair counterfeit.[3]

As no other of the scaly cherubs below seemed to yearn for the same honor, we pulled in our lines and headed for the little rocky islet just off the southern foreland of the port. It had no beach and its craggy gnarly sides went sheer down into the crystal depths. A low, jagged point gave us a landing spot to bundle ashore. We had to watch our chance and jump; and by either miracle or luck the feat was accomplished without broken bones or a souse in the sea. We found the little island supporting a denser population to the square acre than London or even Canton; bipeds, too, though of another family, enjoying life as much and attending as

[3]Vol. II, plate III: description, p. 257. [See photo, p. 163.]

strictly to business. Most of the inhabitants were solemnly sitting on their eggs; a monotonous life I fancy, though I never tried it, but rewarded with ample dividends. They showed no signs of fear, which I am ashamed to say was because they did not know us. And we strolled among battalions of gannets and seagulls and shags so densely crowded that we could scarcely move without stepping on them, leisurely examining their plumage and even handling their eggs. They, meanwhile, kept up a subdued gossip and chatter, which, I suppose, was their way of expressing their opinion of their outlandish guests. It ought to have been favorable, for we came away without killing a bird but left them to their peaceful labors of populating the cliffs and waves with no fear of Malthus before their eyes. That was the nearest I ever came to attendance at Chaucer's *Assembly of Foules*.

I have credited the Bonins with a score of occupants. To be strictly accurate, there were thirty-one: including three or four Americans and three or four Englishmen, and one native of sunny Portugal; Kanaka wives* and half-breed children made up the sum total. The head chief of the island, so far as there was any head, was a man named Savary, a waif from Massachusetts. In token of his primacy the commodore presented him with an American flag, which was run up at once on the flagstaff over his

*Kanaka, a generic term for any Polynesian native, was applied throughout the Pacific Ocean region.—Ed.

Sewall refers to an outing when one of these fish was caught (see page 161); from The Expedition of an American Squadron, Volume II

Courtesy University of Chicago Library

bungalow among the trees. It was a pleasant sight for the first thing in the morning to greet our eyes when we came on deck. Peel Island was the only one of the group occupied; the citizens of the others were wild hogs and goats. The settlers lived a quiescent, semicivilized, subtropical life, cultivating a few acres, raising their own sugar and tobacco, obtaining other commodities from the outer world by barter with occasional passing ships, to which they furnished such natural supplies of wood and water and food as the island could afford. During our stay, three whalers appeared off the port and sent in their boats for the purpose. In all this half century since, I have met but one person who has ever visited this out-of-the-way group. That was a former teacher in Yokohama, now the wife of a banker in America.

On one of her voyages to Japan the ship in which she was a passenger was driven by a typhoon to take refuge in Port Lloyd. While there, she made the acquaintance of the settlers, especially the house of Savary; later a little granddaughter of the white chief was for some years a pupil in her school at Yokohama. At the time of her visit, the Japanese government had assumed control and formed a colony; and there were then already some five hundred Japanese in residence. The old independent solitude so dear to the original barbaric rovers had vanished, and the islands were beginning to hum with the common activities of life. While writing these pages, I have by accident discovered one of their industries. Having occasion to open a can for the household, it gave me an agreeable shock to find it was canned turtle from the Bonins.

We left these charming islands Saturday morning, the eighteenth of June. The last thing I did on shore was to fill my pockets with lumps of chalcedony that lay scattered among the pebbles on the beach. As I was showing my treasures on board, some of them beautiful specimens, one of the wardroom officers who had entered the navy as a middy in his boyhood and so had gleaned his education not from schools but from general experience in knocking about the world, said eagerly, "Now, Clerk, some of these stones ought to be polished and set; as soon as ever you get back to Boston I would take them to a dilapidary!" Bless his heart, that was just what I did. And the "dilapidary" did such fine work that one of my lady friends prizes her chalcedony pin and cuff buttons to this day.

Five days later we were at anchor again in Napa harbor, ready now for the final move on Japan.

VII

The Famous Perry Expedition to Japan

AT LAST, on the second of July 1853, four of the fleet got underway for Japan. The *Saratoga* took her place in tow of the *Susquehanna* as before, and the *Plymouth* in tow of the *Mississippi*. The *Supply* storeship was left for the time at anchor in Napa harbor, and the *Caprice*, under command of Lieutenant William L. Maury, was sent to Shanghai. Our course followed the chain of island groups that extend to the northward and eastward from Lew Chew over to Nippon—some of the time in sight of them. One of the last we passed was Ohosima, a well-bred volcano that was enjoying a nice quiet smoke all by itself. It may wake up someday and start its furnaces, as its fiery neighbor Torisima has been doing while these pages have been in process of incubation. There is plenty of time; geology will furnish all it wants. And it may yet make its record in history and hold up its head with Vesuvius and Krakatoa and Mont Pelée. They are uncertain characters, these volcanoes; you can never be quite sure when any given island is preparing to burn out its chimney. The safest plan is to follow Confucius's advice about the gods—"Respect them, and keep out of their way."

We made moderate speed and reached Japan on the eighth of July. It was Friday, a memorable day in our calendar. That morning the lookouts at the masthead echoed through the fleet the rousing call, "Land ho!" We rushed on deck. There it was, at last. There it was, a dark silent cloud on the northern horizon, a *terra incognita* still shrouded in mystery, still inspiring the imagination with an indefinable awe, just as it had years ago in the studies of our childhood at school. We came up with it rapidly. But the rugged headlands and capes still veiled themselves in mist, as if resolved upon secrecy to the last. About noon the fog melted away, and there lay spread before us the Empire of the Rising Sun, a living picture of hills and valleys, of fields and hedges, groves, orchards, and forests that tufted the lawns and mantled the heights, villages with streets just a trifle wider, and houses a little less densely packed than those in China, defended by forts mounted with howitzers and "quakers," and fenced with long stripes of black and white cotton, which signified that the fortifications were garrisoned and ready for business. On the waters were strange boats skimming about, impelled by strange boatmen, uncouth junks wafted slowly along by the breeze, vanishing behind the promontories and reappearing in the distance, or lowering their sails and dropping their four-fluked anchors in the harbors near us. And towering above all, forty miles inland, like a giant man-at-arms standing sentry over

U.S.S. Susquehanna

Courtesy Special Collections Division, The Nimitz Library, United States Naval Academy, Annapolis, Maryland

Japanese Junk; from The Expedition of an American Squadron

Courtesy The Beverly R. Robinson Collection, United States Naval Academy Museum, Annapolis, Maryland

the scene, rose the snowy peak of Fusiyama, an extinct volcano fourteen thousand feet high, one of the most shapely cones in the world and well named "the matchless mountain."

Our squadron comprised, as already noted, two steam frigates and two sloops of war. For equipment we mustered sixty-one guns and 977 officers and men—a respectable force for the times, but soon eclipsed and forgotten in the vaster armaments of the Civil War and of our late scrimmage with Spain. Such a warlike apparition in the bay, small as it was, created a powerful sensation. A Japanese writer informs us that "the popular commotion in Yedo . . . was beyond description. The whole city was in an uproar. In all directions were seen mothers flying with children in their arms and men with mothers on their backs. Rumors of an immediate action, exaggerated each time they were communicated from mouth to mouth, added horror to the horror-stricken. The tramp of war-horses, the clatter of armed warriors, the noise of carts, the parade of firemen, the incessant tolling of bells, the shrieks of women, the cries of children, dinning all the streets of a city of more than a million souls, made confusion worse confounded."[1]

Of all this we were quite unconscious. We had no idea that we had frightened the empire so badly, the capital being some forty or fifty miles away from

[1]Nitobe. *Intercourse between the United States and Japan*, p. 46.

our anchorage. But that the town near us was thrown into convulsions by the big "black fireships of the barbarians," as the Japanese called us, was sufficiently evident. Before our anchors were fairly down, a battery on Cape Kamisaki sent a trio of bombshells to inquire after our health, or perhaps to consign us to perdition. But they exploded harmlessly astern, and we sent no bombshells back to explain how we were, or whether we intended going in the direction indicated. Our friends on shore knew something of guns and gunnery—that was plain. How much, we could not tell. But our glasses showed us that not all the black logs frowning at us from their portholes were genuine. Some at least were "quakers," that could not be fired except in a general conflagration; like the battery of a native guard boat in the harbor of Nagasaki that once upon a time capsized in a squall; various things went to the bottom, but most of her guns floated!

By the time we were well anchored and sails furled and men piped down, swarms of picturesque Mandarins came off to challenge the strange arrival and to draw around the fleet the customary cordon of guard boats. This looked like being in custody. The American ambassador had not come to Japan to be put under sentries. He notified the Mandarins that his vessels were not pirates and need not be watched. They pleaded Japanese law. He replied with American law. They still insisted. Whereupon he clinched the American side of the argument with the notice that if the boats were not off in fifteen minutes, he should be obliged to open his batteries and sink them. That was entirely convincing, and the guard boats stood not on the order of their going but betook themselves to the shelter of the shore.

I well remember that still starlit night that closed our first day in Yedo Bay. Nothing disturbed its peaceful beauty. The towering ships slept motionless on the water, and the twinkling lights of the towns along the shore went out one by one. A few beacon fires lighted upon the hilltops, the rattling cordage of an occasional passing junk, the musical tones of a distant temple bell that came rippling over the bay at intervals throughout the long night—these were to us the only tokens of life in the sleeping empire.

A sleeping empire truly; aloof from the world, shut in within itself and utterly severed from the general world-consciousness, not awake to the opportunities and privileges it was later so suddenly and so brilliantly to achieve as one of the world's powers, not even conscious that there was any such high position to be attained. While the expedition is resting at its anchors, and the empire around is asleep, let us take the chance to paint in a bit of the background. An historical reminiscence or two will enable us more fully to appreciate the aim and the ultimate success of the enterprise.

The Sunrise Kingdom, like the telescope, was discovered by accident. In 1542, when Henry VIII of England, Charles V of Germany, Knox, Calvin, and Luther were the chief characters on the European stage, a Portuguese vessel bound to Macao in China was driven by storms into Bungo, a port of Kiusiu. It was the first meeting of Japanese and Europeans. It seems to have been mutually agreeable. The accidental visitors were dazzled with the riches of the oriental paradise they had found, and the natives were pleased and entertained with their outlandish guests. When the news reached Europe, it started a crusade of adventurers to the eastern seas. There was gold fever; all the commercial nations of the West had even caught it. The flags of Portugal, England, Holland, France, and Spain soon waved in succession over the waters of the newly discovered empire. The Japanese were amiable, and a busy barter was maintained for some scores of years.

Traders and speculators were not the only visitors in that distant mart. Some ten years later the Jesuits resolved to signalize the beginnings of their new order by converting those rich and dissolute Gentiles. Their crusade, like many others, was successful. It is related that when the first missioners, as they were called, reached the field of their operations, some of the courtiers desired an edict against the propagation of the new faith. "How many religions have we now?" asked the emperor. "Thirty-five," was the answer. "Very well," said the tolerant monarch, "One more will hurt nobody–let them preach." And they did preach. And Xavier, the renowned Jesuit apostle and saint, though within the year he returned to China to die, lived long enough to baptize multitudes of the penitent pagans, grandees as well as commoners and peasantry. Other missioners flocked to the harvest. The Jesuits were then followed by Dominicans and Franciscans. The splendid robes and ritual of the church proved attractive and large numbers of the people were gathered into the Roman fold. Shrines were deserted and priests found their custom wasting away.

This was a result not entirely palatable to either the priesthood or the court. Several of the emperors recalled their apostate subjects to the mourning gods. Persecutions began. The foreign monks and friars were accused of political intrigue. The story is a bloody one and covers a whole generation of tragedy and horror. Let us turn the page and simply record the fact that Christianity was expunged from Japan.

The final catastrophe occurred in 1637 at the fall of Simabara and the massacre of some forty thousand Christians. The histories tell us that the bodies of the martyrs were tumbled together into one vast pit and over it was raised this defiant inscription: "So long as the sun shall warm the earth let no Christian be so bold as to come to Japan; and let all know that the King of Spain himself, or the Christian's God, or the most great God of all, if he violate this command, shall pay for it with his head."[2] Then the murderous empire wiped its sword, shut its gates, and barred itself in against all the world. One of the precautions by which it protected itself against Christianity and the civilization of the West was the famous ceremony of trampling on the cross; the astute pagans rightly divining that no foreigner would consent to such a sacrilege who had enough of the Christian religion about him to disturb the empire.

The ceremony was performed every year, as methodically as taking the census or collecting the taxes, and was only abolished as late as 1853, after our first visit to Japan.[3] Once a year, officers went to every house with boxes containing the crucifix and images of the Virgin. These were laid on the floor, and all the household from octogenarians to infants in arms were required to tread upon them as a proof that they were not Christians. This law was enforced among the Dutch, the only western nation that maintained its foothold in the hermit land during all those darkened centuries. It is said that the cross was carved into the stone thresholds of their warehouses so that they could neither go nor come without trampling upon it. The placid Hollanders do not seem to have been much distressed by the requirement; their convenient religion was easily detached and left in Europe. One of them, we are

[2]MacFarlane, *Japan*, pp. 49–50.
[3]Griffis, *Matthew Calbraith Perry*, p. 349.

told, one day wandered away from the warehouses on the island of Dezima across the bridge into the streets of Nagasaki and was suddenly halted by a Japanese patrol. "Are you a Christian?" was the challenge. "No, I am a Dutchman!" He was allowed to pass.

It is time to return to the ships. We left them sound asleep at anchor off Uraga the night of our arrival in Yedo Bay. Yet not all sound asleep, for a more vigilant watch has rarely been kept than was kept that night on board that fleet. Nothing happened however–except a brilliant display of meteoric light in the sky during the midwatch, an omen that terribly alarmed our friends on shore as portending that the very heavens themselves were enlisted on the side of these foreign barbarians. The commodore alludes to the phenomenon in his narrative and adds the devout wish, "The ancients would have construed this remarkable appearance of the heavens as a favorable omen for any enterprise they had undertaken; it may be so construed by us, as we pray God that our present attempt to bring a singular and isolated people into the family of civilized nations may succeed without resort to bloodshed."[4] In spite of the menacing sky we all survived, Yankees and natives, and in the morning were all alive and ready for business.

During the day, our new friends came off to visit the ships and some were admitted on board. These

[4]Official *Narrative of the Expedition*, &c. I: 236.

first interviews were a constant surprise to us; we found them so well-informed. They questioned us about the Mexican War, then recent; about General Taylor and General Santa Anna.* On board the *Susquehanna* one day, a Japanese gentleman asked the officer of the deck, "Where did you come from?" "From America," the officer replied. "Yes, I know," he said, "Your whole fleet came from the United States. But this ship–did she come from New York? or Philadelphia? or Washington?" He knew enough of our geography not to locate our seaports on our western prairies or up among the Rockies–a pitch of intelligence not yet too common among even our European friends. One of them asked if the monster gun on the quarter-deck was a "paixhan" gun?** Yes, it was, but where and how could he ever have heard the name? When two or three midshipmen were taking the sun at noon, one of them laid his sextant down and a Japanese taking it up remarked that such instruments came from London and Paris and the best were made in London. How could a Japanese know that?

Our colloquies were carried on in Dutch through our Dutch interpreter, Mr. Portman, the educated

*For General Zachary Taylor and General Antonio Lopez de Santa Anna, see the Lakeside Classic by George Ballentine, *Autobiography of an English Soldier in the United States Army*, edited by William H. Goetzmann (Chicago: R.R. Donnelley & Sons Company, 1986).–Ed.

**A gun named for its French inventor, General Henri Joseph Paixhans (1783–1854).–Ed.

Japanese being then accustomed to the use of that language somewhat as we use French. We naturally supposed, therefore, that all their information had come through the Dutch, the only nation beside the neighboring Chinese and Koreans that had for the last three centuries kept its hold upon the good graces and the commerce of Japan. But we afterwards found that the Japanese printers were in the habit of republishing the textbooks prepared by our missionaries in China for use in their schools. The knowledge of America which we found thus diffused in Japan had come straight from Dr. Bridgman's *History of the United States*, a manual written and published in China, which also had, what the good doctor never dreamed of, a wide circulation in the realm of the Mikado.* That book had already prepossessed its readers in our favor. The following winter it was my privilege to make the acquaintance of the author at his home in Shanghai and to sit often at his genial board. It has been one of the regrets of my life that I could not tell him and his accomplished wife that his little textbook was speeding its way within the Empire of the Rising Sun. But at that time, alas, none of us knew it. They have both long since gone home to the heaven they loved, and probably never learned in this world of the good they had thus unconsciously done.

*Elijah Coleman Bridgman (1801–61), the first American Protestant missionary to China; he arrived in 1830 and served there until his death.—Ed.

The next day was Sunday. According to custom, divine service was held on board the flagship. The capstan on the quarterdeck was draped with the flag and the Bible was laid open upon it. Chaplain Jones took his station beside it. I do not know that any record was made of the service; presumably the chaplain followed the usual liturgical form and preached a brief sermon. But the hymn sung on the occasion has become historic; it was Watts' solemn lyric:

"Before Jehovah's awful throne,
Ye nations, bow with sacred joy."

It was sung to the tune of "Old Hundred" and was led by the full band. The familiar strains poured in mighty chorus from two hundred or three hundred lusty throats with a peal that echoed through the fleet and wafted the gracious message to the distant shore. The Japanese listened with wonder; and their wonder deepened into amazement when they found that the whole day was to be observed as a day of rest and none of them could be admitted on board.[5]

On Monday the secular tide was turned on again and diplomatic overtures began in good earnest. In their official dealings with us it was interesting to see how the authorities clung to their time-honored policy of exclusion. It was a curious contest of steady nerve on one side, met by the most nimble

[5]Griffis, *Matthew Calbraith Perry*, p. 324. Official *Narrative of the Expedition*, &c. I: 240

First Landing at Gorahama; from The Expedition of an American Squadron

Courtesy University of Chicago Library

parrying on the other. First they directed the commodore to go home; they wanted no letters from American presidents, nor any treaty. But the commodore would not go home. Then they ordered him to Nagasaki, where foreign business could be properly transacted through the Dutch. But the commodore declined to go to Nagasaki. If then this preposterous barbarian would not budge, and his letter must be received, they would receive it without ceremony on board ship. But his Western mightiness would not deliver it on board ship. Then they asked for time to consult the court at Yedo, and the commodore gave them three days—days big with fate; but exactly what happened at court we may never know. This much is certain, that our reluctant friends yielded at last; that pestilent letter would be received, and commissioners of suitable rank would come from court for the purpose. Even after all preliminaries had been settled, they begged to receive the letter on board ship, not on shore. But the Rubicon had been passed.

Some three miles below our anchorage a little semicircular harbor makes in on the western side of the bay, and at the head of it stands the village or hamlet of Kurihama. That was the spot selected for the meeting of the Western envoy and the imperial commissioners, and there the Japanese erected a temporary hall of audience. It was a memorable scene. The two frigates steamed slowly down and anchored off the harbor. How big, black, and sullen they looked, masterful, accustomed to having their own way, full of pent-up force. Our little flotilla of fifteen boats landed under cover of their guns. We were not quite three hundred all told, but well befeathered in full uniform and armed to the teeth; a somewhat impressive lot, and yet of rather scant dimensions to confront five thousand native troops drawn up on the beach to receive us, with crowds of curious spectators lining the housetops and grouped on the hills in the rear. However, we were ready for anything and had no fear of treachery. The emblazonry of those Japanese regiments surpasses any powers of description that have been vouchsafed to the present deponent. Their radiant uniforms and trappings and ensigns must have been cut out of rainbows and sunsets; and the scores of boats fringing the shore heightened the effect with their fluttering plumage of flags. There was one thing not lively; the officers of these gorgeous troops sat in silent dignity on campstools in front of the line—a kind of military coma that the hustling regiments now tackling the great Northern Bear in Manchuria evidently have not inherited and could not comprehend.*

The situation was unique, not likely to be forgotten by any who participated in it, either American or Japanese. It was a clear and calm summer morning. As our lines disembarked and formed on

*Northern Bear signifies Russia, and "tackling" dates are Sewall's reference to the Russo-Japanese War of 1904–05.—Ed.

Commodore Perry Meeting Imperial Commissioners at Yokohama; from
The Expedition of an American Squadron

Courtesy The Beverly R. Robinson Collection, United States Naval Academy Museum, Annapolis, Maryland

the beach, the commodore stepped into his barge to follow us. Instantly the black "fireships" were wrapped in white clouds of smoke, and the thunder of their salute echoed among the hills and groves back of the village. To the startled spectators on shore they must have seemed suddenly transformed into floating volcanoes. And when the great man landed, they gazed with wonder, for no mortal eye (no Japanese mortal) had been permitted to look upon him before. In all the negotiations hitherto he had played their own game and veiled himself in mystery. They could communicate with so lofty a being only through his subordinates. This was not child's play. It was not an assumption of pomp inconsistent with republican simplicity. Commodore Perry was dealing with an oriental potentate according to oriental ideas. He showed his sagacity in doing so. At this time he was fifty-nine years old, a man of splendid physique and commanding presence. He had already lived through a varied experience that had helped to train him for this culminating achievement of his life. Endowed with strong native powers he had risen in mental capacity and executive force with every stage of his professional career.

The War of 1812, in which also his famous brother Oliver Hazard* and two younger brothers

*Oliver Hazard Perry, U.S.N. (1785–1819), victor over the British in the Battle of Lake Erie in 1813. His report, "We have met the enemy and they are ours," made him famous.—Ed.

served, gave him his first baptism of fire; and later the Mexican War, service in various parts of the world civilized and savage, duties on naval boards at home, investigations and experiments in naval science, naval architecture, naval education—these and numberless other methods of serving his country both in the professional routine and in general affairs, had developed his judgment, his mental acumen, his breadth of vision, his knowledge of men; and thus had prepared him for his high mission as ambassador and diplomat. Unquestionably his insight into the oriental mind, his firmness and persistence, his stalwart physical presence, his portly bearing, his dignity, his poise, his stately courtesy were prime factors in his success as a negotiator with an Eastern court. He was the right kind of man for America to send on such an errand to such a people.

On his arrival we marched to the hall through an avenue of soldiers, our escort being formed of sailors and marines from the four ships. Leaving the escort drawn up on the beach, the forty officers entered. We found ourselves within a broad canopied court of cotton hangings, carpeted with white, overlaid in the center with a scarlet breadth for a pathway leading to and extending up on the raised floor of the hall beyond. Many two-sworded officials in state robes were kneeling on either side of this flaming track. Within the hall sat—not in Japanese fashion but on chairs—the imperial commissioners, the

Delivery of the President's Letter; from The Expedition of an American Squadron

Courtesy The Beverly R. Robinson Collection, United States Naval Academy Museum, Annapolis, Maryland

princes Idzu and Iwami,* surrounded by their kneeling suite. They were both men of some years, fifty or sixty perhaps; Idzu a pleasant intellectual-looking man, Iwami's features narrow and somewhat disfigured by the smallpox; both were attired in magnificent robes richly embroidered in silver and gold. Vacant seats opposite the commissioners were taken by the commodore and his staff. Between the lines were the interpreters, on one side a native scholar on his knees, on the other erect and dignified the official interpreter of the squadron, S. Wells Williams LL.D., a well-known author and missionary in China. Behind them stood a scarlet lacquered chest that was destined to receive the fateful missive for conveyance to court. Overhead in rich folds drooped the purple silk hangings profusely decorated with the imperial arms and the national bird, the stork.

I had scarcely noted these few details and glanced at the genial face of Bayard Taylor as he stood behind the commodore taking notes, when the ceremony began. It was very brief. A few words between the interpreters, and then, at a signal, two boys in blue entered followed then by two stalwart Negroes, probably the first to be seen on the landscape of Japan. In slow and impressive fashion the two men brought in the rosewood boxes that contained the mysterious papers. These were

*The former is now transliterated in shorter form as Prince Izu; the latter's name remains unaltered as Prince Iwami.—Ed.

opened in silence and laid on the scarlet coffer. Prince Iwami handed to the interpreters a formal receipt for the documents. The commodore announced that he should return the next spring for the reply. A brief conversation in answer to a question about the progress of the Taiping Rebellion in China, and the conference closed, having lasted not more than twenty minutes. A short ceremony, and witnessed by not more than fifty or sixty persons out of the entire populations of both the great countries engaged; but it was the opening of Japan. It brought together as neighbors and friends two nations that were the antipodes of each other not only in position on the globe but in almost every element of their two types of civilization.

That the Japanese have themselves appreciated the significance of this memorable meeting appears in the amazing historical developments that have followed all over the empire along the lines of commerce, industrial art, education, and religion, and is shown also by innumerable public utterances from the platform and press; and they have recently commemorated the occasion by erecting a monument at Kurihama in honor of the American commodore. But this later material can wait until the end of the chapter; we will keep on here with the main story.

This first act of the mission was now achieved, and the squadron rested from its labors. A great weight was lifted off its mind. The next day, with

The Prince of Idzu; from The Expedition of an American Squadron

Courtesy The Beverly R. Robinson Collection, United States Naval Academy Museum, Annapolis, Maryland

lightened conscience, it set itself to the easier task of surveying and sounding the bay, exploring future harbors, locating islands and rocks, measuring distances, and plotting charts. These uncanny operations were watched with some solicitude by the coast guards. They offered no active opposition, though once or twice we had occasion to show how thoroughly each boat was armed and ready for emergencies. The *Saratoga*, not willing to be outdone in this hydrographic work, located one shoal with undoubted accuracy by running upon it full tilt. Fortunately the wind was light and the bottom smooth; no harm was done to either ship or shoal. We were not proud of the achievement; but the commodore did us the honor to immortalize it and us by naming the sandbar the "Saratoga Spit"; and that title it bears to this day. Some years later it acquired a tragic interest when the U.S.S. *Oneida*, coming down the bay to sail for home, was run into in the night and sunk by the British mailship *Bombay*. She went down close by the "Saratoga Spit," carrying with her most of her hapless crew.

A few days after the Kurihama conference we left the Empire of the Rising Sun and returned to the Central Flowery Kingdom. On the seventeenth of July, as silently as they had entered nine days before, the two frigates steamed out of the bay with the two ships in tow. Outside they separated and went their several ways; the two steamers and the *Plymouth* back to Lew Chew and the *Saratoga* to

Shanghai. We parted in a storm. If our Japanese friends could have seen our belabored ships scuttling away into the darkness and foam they would have taken it for a special interposition of their wind-god, wreaking vengeance on the Western barbarians for their temerity. The gale grew into a tempest, and the tempest into a typhoon, the largest though not the most vicious of the four encountered by the *Saratoga* in those uneasy seas. We compared the logbooks afterward of several ships that were caught in different sections of its enormous circuit and found that it was more than 1,000 miles in diameter and, in its progress, swept over the larger part of the north Pacific Ocean. It raged for several days, and every vessel in our fleet got entangled in some part of its vortex. Our own ship, the *Saratoga*, was under orders for Shanghai; and after the gale struck us, with battened hatches and sea-swept decks, we rode on the outer rim of that cyclone almost all the way back into the mouth of the Yang-tse-keang. It was riding a wild steed, as all sailors know who have tried it, but we got to Shanghai all the quicker. Six months we lay there at anchor off the American consulate. It was the time of the Taiping Rebellion. As if to give us further object lessons in the oriental way of making history, one night the Taipings inside the walls rose and captured the city. The imperialist forces came down from Peking to retake it. And about once in three days we were treated to a Chinese battle—

sometimes an assault by land, sometimes a bombardment by the fleet of forty or fifty junks; all very dramatic and spectacular, occasionally tragic, frequently funny. But, as Kipling says, that is another story and deserves a chapter of its own.

Meanwhile here is the place for a codicil in which to record the Kurihama celebration just referred to. During the autumn of 1900, Rear Admiral Beardslee, retired and traveling in Japan, took occasion to revisit the scene of the famous landing. In 1853 he was a young midshipman on board the *Plymouth*, and was in charge of one of the boats of the flotilla. He easily identified the spot and finding it neglected brought it to the attention of the *Beiyu-Kwai*–"Society of Friends of America"– who assumed the patriotic task of renovating the place and commemorating the event. The occasion truly was an inspiring one. On 14 July 1901, which was the forty-eighth anniversary of the conference, and on the spot where the hall of conference stood, there assembled a distinguished company of dignitaries of the empire, the officials of the *Beiyu-Kwai*, Admiral Beardslee and other representative Americans, together with many thousand interested spectators. Baron Kaneko presided and addressed the company. Other addresses followed, from the American minister Colonel Buck, from Viscount Katsura, from Admirals Rodgers and Beardslee, U.S.N., and also from the Governor of Kanagawa. It was felicitous circumstance that when the supreme moment came the monument was unveiled by Admiral Rodgers, a grandson of Commodore Perry and at that time commanding the American squadron in the East. The memorial is a shaft of unpolished granite standing on a massive base and rising to a height over all of thirty-three feet. The side facing the bay bears this inscription in Japanese:

> This monument marks the landing place of
> Commodore Perry of the United States of
> North America. Marquis Ito Hirobumi,
> Highest Order of Merit.

On the reverse is an inscription in English:

> This monument commemorates the
> first arrival of Commodore Perry,
> Ambassador from the United States of America,
> who landed at this place July 14, 1853.
> Erected July 14, 1901.

This solid memorial will forever dignify the little Japanese hamlet of Kurihama as the birthplace of the new Japan and the scene of the beginnings of a great international friendship.

In this epilogue belongs also the record of another celebration more recent and of a more personal flavor. The Japanese in foreign lands have a patriotic custom of strengthening the home ties by celebrating the birthday of their emperor, which falls on the third of November. The year 1903 marked a half century from the first landing of the Perry expedition on Japanese soil, and Mr. Uchida, the Japanese consul-general in New York, con-

American Boy Scouts at the Commodore Perry Monument at Kurihama During the Black Ship Festival in 1953

Courtesy UPI/Bettmann Archive

ceived the happy idea of adding still further prestige to the usual celebration by commemorating that famous event. Invitations were issued to the descendants of Commodore Perry and to the now few survivors of the fleet. Out of the more than two thousand officers and men who composed the personnel of the expedition, less than a score are known to be living, three of whom were present at the reception.

To these three, who had not met for half a century, it may well be imagined the occasion was impressive, not to say thrilling. The forty or fifty Japanese gentlemen and the ladies present, and as many more Americans, some of them descendants of the famous commodore, and others who had been resident in the Mikado's dominions or were specially interested in the country and its people, made a most brilliant assemblage. The memories were indeed inspiring.

The half century had enlarged the dimensions of the event; rather had brought out and developed its natural results along the lines of trade, industrial art, commerce, education, intellectual and moral enlightenment, and so splendidly that the growing light reflected back on the original act and revealed its magnitude. With these sentiments were also mingled tender thoughts of shipmates long since gone and memories of scenes that made us sigh:

> –for the touch of a vanished hand,
> And the sound of a voice that is still.

On the walls hung a large old-time colored lithograph representing the landing at Kurihama, a print struck off soon after the return of the fleet and loaned for the occasion by one of the commodore's daughters. Near it was a companion picture of the same size, a photograph of the Perry monument at Kurihama.

After the social hour, the consul called his guests to order and made an address of welcome, alluding to the emperor, the expedition, and the presence of some who had been members of it. Two other brief speeches were made, one by Admiral Rodgers, a grandson of the old commodore, who spoke of his grandfather's mission in Japan, his own service in the East, and the unveiling of the Kurihama monument. The other was by one of the survivors and was, of course, largely reminiscent of those distant scenes and descriptive of our famous old commander. It gives one a funny sensation to stand before a brilliant company as a relic of some ancient bit of history, and be watched by such curious eyes while you step out of your own past generation into the light of modern times to make your speech!

When the tables were brought in for the banquet, it fell to us three "relics" with three or four friends to surround the same board–a sumptuous improvement on a middies' mess in the steerage of a man-of-war and seasoned with high memories. As we broke bread together and the current of converse moved swiftly on, it seemed almost as if we were surrounded by the unseen forms of messmates who had long since sailed on to the haven beyond. And back of all was the thought of the Sunrise Kingdom herself, the hermit land of half a century ago, so exclusive, so mysterious, but now so teeming with the activities of a new civilization, the resources of a new power, and all the dignity and responsibility of a new place in the world. The occasion itself, the sentiments it inspired, and the distinguished company uniting in the celebration, all combined to make it a memorable evening.

VIII

The Taipings in Shanghai: An Episode of the Great Rebellion

FROM JAPAN to China is not a long voyage, if you ride on the rim of a cyclone. The memories linger still of a rusty and belabored man-of-war wearily crawling up the waves and then plunging down in roar and foam, rolling almost on her beam ends and burying her batteries alternately out of sight; the air full of driving spray, wind shrieking through the rigging, sails flapping to pieces, hatches battened down, everything tumbling, chaotic, dismal and wet. At last the tempest chased us into the turbid waters of the Yang-tse-keang and sheered off down the coast in quest of easier prey.

It does not strike one like a river—the Yang-tse-keang—but a broad gulf, whose low alluvial shores are far and away out of sight of each other. Up some sixty miles, you turn south into a branch, the Wusung, and thread your way up through a motley fleet of foreign ships, opium hulks, lorchas, junks, tanka boats, sampans, and other Celestial craft. By the aid of a Chinese pilot, a little wind, storms of pidgin-English, and diverse bumpings with awkward junks, you traverse some fifteen miles more and come to your moorings off the city of Shanghai.

At least that was the way the *Saratoga* got there

in August 1853. We dropped anchor off the foreign quarter. It was a scene of busy prosperity. First of all, the Bund, an esplanade lined with residences facing the river as if on parade, clean broad streets, warehouses and godowns stored with the products of the empire; and, over all, the protective flags of the consulates—English, American, Spanish, and French. Farther up the river to the south lay the Chinese city behind a wall twenty feet high and a moat twenty feet wide, environed even on the river side with suburbs as dense and crowded as the streets within; its houses jammed and dovetailed together like the pieces in a puzzle; its thoroughfares too narrow for any but pedestrians and sedans; its atmosphere redolent of those pungent aromatic odors which no visitor in the great empire could ever mistake or ever forget—or in the Central Flowery Kingdom landscape has not only form and color but smell; its somber level of gray tiles overtopped and relieved by the French Catholic cathedral in the southeastern quarter, the spire of an American Episcopal mission near the center, and a forest of masts rising from an indescribable chaos of junks along the riverfront.

The city stands within the forks of the Wusung and the Hwangpu, which here unite and carry their common burden forward into the Yang-tse-keang. The Hwangpu brings down from Suchau and other great inland marts hundreds and thousands of country barges laden to the water's edge with the

Chinese Barber in Macao; from The Expedition of an American Squadron

Chinese Girl with Head Dress; from The Expedition of an American Squadron

Illustrations Courtesy University of Chicago Library

produce of field, garden, shop, and loom. The Wusung, though with its best endeavors less than half a mile wide, accommodates the heaviest merchantmen as well as immense fleets of native craft that swarm hither to share and swell the enormous traffic in rice, tea, and silk. A snapshot from the quarterdeck in the cool of the afternoon, if kodaks had arrived on this planet in those faraway days, would have given one a lively mixture: lumbering tea-boats, freight-hoys, yachts, sampans, arrow-like shells out for pleasure or practice, and all manner of shipping from almost every maritime power under the sun. On shore a still livelier turmoil—a bustling Mongolian pandemonium of Orient and Occident commingled. Byron's picture of a carnival in Venice would answer quite well for the motley array one encounters on the Shanghai Bund:

> And there are dresses, splendid but fantastical,
> Masks of all times and nations, Turks and Jews,
> And harlequins and clowns, with feats gymnastical,
> Greeks, Romans, Yankee Doodles and Hindoos.

We had been there but a month in the midst of these busy conditions when suddenly, like the proverbial thunderbolt out of a clear sky, something happened. Things do have a way of happening in China. Of late it has been the Boxers.* Then it was

*The "Boxers," adherents of the Society of Righteous and Harmonious Fists, pursued political and religious ends rampaging across northern China in the summer of 1900 against foreigners and Christians. For the Opium and Sino-Japanese wars, see Dudden, *The American Pacific*, pp. 6–8, 119.—Ed.

the Taipings.* Outbreaks of popular violence in the Great Flowery Kingdom have been frequent and in many ways show a common origin, as well as a family likeness. The Opium War of 1842, the Taiping Rebellion, the French and English invasion of 1857–60, the recent eruption of the Boxers, even the collision with Japan in 1893–94, may all be credited in a general way, as they have been, to the irrepressible conflict between two types of civilizations. Wherever the sea meets the shore, there is a foaming line of surf. And wherever the advancing tide of Western life meets the solid mass of Mongolian conservatism, the impact produces more or less of tumult.

In the case of the Opium War, China was trying to choke out the fatal drug from the empire, and England, to her lasting shame, was making reprisals for the loss and fastening the curse upon the unwilling victim. The uprising of the Boxers was a savage attempt to sweep all foreigners from the sacred soil and bar the gates against the polluting contact of the Western world. The Taiping Rebellion was a more tremendous tragedy than either and had for its aim a blind and blundering endeavor to overthrow the Manchu dynasty. Unlike as these conflicts have been, they were the effervescence of the same chronic spirit of repugnance

*For the Taiping Rebellion (1850–64), to establish The Heavenly Kingdom of Great Peace, see the Editor's Note opening Chapter III.–Ed.

American Consulate in Shanghai; from The Expedition of an American Squadron

Courtesy University of Chicago Library

against foreign interference or even contact, which secretly ferments in the Celestial mind.

There can be no doubt however that by these bloody stages, China is making progress. The empire is slowly leavening with the forces of the new century. In return for the great ideas and inventions she had long since given to the world, some of them hoary and moss-grown with antiquity, the world is now forcing upon her the new and larger methods of life which have developed in the swifter nations of the West. A rapid evolution is going on in her commerce, in her modes of business, in railroad and telegraph, in new lines of manufacture, even in her military methods. Modern armor is usurping the place of the old jingals and spears. Some of her battalions have had the benefit of foreign drill. The empire had a lesson pounded into her in her quarrel with Japan, and another lesson from the powers on the subject of Boxers. She will remember them both. In the garrison captured by Admiral Seymour near Tientsin was found war material of the latest make and of enormous quantity–a sight to open Western eyes. And the viceroy of Hankow is not the only Celestial patriot who has seen far enough ahead to establish vast plants for the making of modern guns and ammunition.

The contrast between the war apparatus these plants are turning out and the antiquated weapons we saw the Taipings using half a century ago would be ludicrous if it were not so startling. If the world keeps on arming these countless millions and drilling them in the latest arts of destruction, and does little or nothing to elevate them in either Christian character or international ethics, an explosion may come big enough to shake all Christendom. The great empire outnumbers the total populations of Europe and America put together; a fact which may well give us pause. For if with modern equipments and European methods the Chinese should discover their power, they might become literally a "yellow peril" to all the rest of the planet.

Taiping means Great Peace, a term not altogether appropriate to the wholesale plundering, ravaging, and slaughtering that were perpetrated under its banners. The full euphemism by which the leader styled himself was "Heavenly Father, Heavenly Elder Brother, Heavenly King of the Great Peace Dynasty of the Heavenly Kingdom." The Heavenly Kingdom means China–little as the unenlightened might suspect it. And though the whole title sounds like a flourish of profanity, it only expresses what the arch-rebel sincerely claimed to be. It was not personal conceit; it was a sober fanatical faith in himself and his mission. Like most disturbers of our planet, the Taiping-wang was a visionary; literally so, for his great ambition began in the visions that glimmered around his sickbed when a young man of twenty-four. He had been in heaven; had met there a "venerable old man" and an "elder brother," with whom he held interviews. They ap-

Engagement with the Taiping Rebels at Nanking by the British Ships
Furious, Retribution, Cruiser, Dove, *and* Lee

Courtesy The Beverly R. Robinson Collection, United States Naval Academy Museum, Annapolis, Maryland

pointed him to his great work on Earth. He held a divine commission from them to conquer and rule China. No personage of less pretensions, and a Chinaman at that, could have asked Sir George Bonham* whether the Virgin Mary had not a pretty sister for him, the Heavenly King, to marry! His visions sustained him through his period of obscurity into the dawn of success, when adherents trooped around him and weary marches issued in brilliant campaigns. Nor did the golden dream utterly fade until in the final crash of defeat and ruin he took his own life in his palace at Nanking.

At first the rebellion had an aim. That was to overturn the Manchu dynasty, which had ruled the empire ever since the conquest in 1644, and restore to the throne a native Chinese prince. The Taiping claimed to be a descendant of the Mings, the last native dynasty that had occupied the Chinese throne. It was also claimed that he had in his possession the banner which distinguished the last emperor of that house. It had been preserved by a sage and handed down with the prediction that he who unfurled and bore it would overturn the hated Manchu and recover the ancient scepter. It had magical virtues, and under this talisman the rebels were surely marching to victory.

With this main purpose was curiously mingled a

*Sir George Bonham (1803–63), British governor of Hong Kong, envoy-extraordinary and minister plenipotentiary and superintendent of trade in China.–Ed.

sort of hybrid Christianity. The Heavenly King had in his youth received instruction from an American missionary.[1] He had carried to his home in the interior some religious tracts prepared by a countryman, Leang Afa. Imbibing the new opinions, he became an eager zealot and iconoclast. Ten commandments were promulgated somewhat like the ten of the Old Testament. A form of worship became part of the camp routine. And wherever they marched, temples were looted and the impotent gods were left strewn in fragments on the ground. The two motives—a rescued country and a new religion—proved attractive. The Taipings were brave soldiers, and, when led by competent chieftains, they performed many deeds that deserve a place in history.

Beginning in the autumn of 1850 near Canton, the revolt grew from a handful to an army, and spread from a single center until it had infected whole provinces. Sweeping rapidly northward the

[1]Rev. Issachar Roberts, a Baptist missionary. I met him in Hong Kong in 1852 and found him enthusiastic in his hopes of the results that would come to his beloved China from such a glorious revolution. At the request of the rebel leader he visited the camp and was warmly welcomed. He remained some months and assisted the Taiping-wang in establishing his novel reforms. Whether it was the unique form of baptism adopted by the rebels in place of immersion—wiping the breast with a wet towel in token of a clean heart—or whether a growing incompatibility of temper between the two leaders, or even graver matters of discord, I cannot say; but his mission came to a sudden end, and he saved his head by disappearing from camp. See Martin, *A Cycle of Cathay*, pp. 131–32.

insurgent forces cut a vast swath through the heart of the empire, mowing down cities, hamlets, towns, everything that came in their way. When Nanking was taken by storm and its defenders put to the sword, the Heavenly King selected the great city for his capital and there set up his banners and his throne. This was in March 1853. The next thing was to reduce Peking. An army was dispatched to the north for that purpose. It never reached Peking; yet the exploit was one that might well deserve the admiration of any soldier of the West. In six months these insurgents marched fifteen hundred miles, traversed four provinces, fought numerous battles and defeated every army sent against them, took twenty-six cities, and won their own subsistence from the country they traversed and the enemy they fought. An American, who spent most of his life in China and who was a contemporary of the great struggle, declares that under the circumstances it was a feat quite equal to Sherman's exploit of ten years later, the famous march to the sea.

The rebellion lasted from 1850 to 1865. In its later years it degenerated into a predatory war, and its armies into hordes of banditti. The Heavenly King, as events proved, had no broad view of his own future, no capacity for organizing government, no large plans for establishing his dynasty of Great Peace, and scarcely a shred left of his mongrel Christianity. It was just a blind remorseless struggle for conquest, trusting to luck or to heavenly visions for a favorable issue. The fantastic costume of his troops, their outlandish flags, their wild hairy aspect (they did not shave their heads) struck terror into the hearts of their enemies; and wherever they went they left their track in ashes and blood. What torments the wretched empire was suffering from both its foes and its defenders may be seen in the fate of Hankow, a populous city which, within a period of some two years, was taken by assault by one army or the other no less than six times, and turned literally into a heap of ruins. Ningpo would furnish an example still more striking. After it had been recaptured by the allied forces, French, British, and Chinese, Captain Dew says in his official report of the action, "I had known Ningpo in its palmy days, when it boasted itself one of the first commercial cities of the empire; but now on this eleventh of May one might have fancied that an angel of destruction had been at work in the city as in the suburbs. All the latter, with their wealthy hongs and thousands of houses, lay leveled; while in the city itself, once the home of half a million people, no trace or vestige of an inhabitant could be seen. Truly it was a city of the dead."[2]

It was estimated by foreigners resident in the empire at the time, that the struggle cost on both sides fully twenty million lives. This frightful aggregate is not to be credited to actual slaughter in battle, nor to the later ravages of wounds and disease. The at-

[2]Williams, *The Middle Kingdom*, II: 609.

tention of the government was of course concentrated on the war. Every available soldier was drawn to the front. Whole provinces were almost depleted of their laborers. That meant wholesale neglect of the Grand Canal. At numberless points, therefore, the abandoned dikes broke down, and immense sections of once populous territory were flooded. And still worse, the refractory Hoang-ho, which has a habit of changing its course every few years and ploughing a new channel to the sea, more than once burst its banks and spread desolation right and left, sweeping farms, flocks, villages, even cities with their hapless occupants, into indiscriminate ruin. These terrible floods, together with the famines that usually followed in their wake, may be accounted responsible for a large proportion, perhaps half, of the twenty million.[3]

It was in this great contest that Chinese Gordon was assigned to a command in the imperial army. As the war dragged on it had become more and more evident that the Great Peace held out no hope for the distracted empire. There was in it no emancipation from the Tartar yoke, no elevation of the masses into freedom, no melting of pagan night into the dawn of a Christian day. Some of us had hoped

[3]Anyone interested in looking up the biography—one might say indeed the autobiography—of this insubordinate river, will find a brief and clear account by Professor Pumpelly in *Smithsonian Contributions to Knowledge,* No. 202 (1866); together with eleven charts that show the different forms the river has taken within the past twenty-five-hundred years.

and believed that we were about to witness the moral and political regeneration of an empire. It had come to be instead a scramble for loot and blood. Every new turn in the progress of the rebellion only added to the disappointment of its more thoughtful friends; and more than one foreign officer entered the imperial army to aid in stamping out the horror. General Ward,[4] who had served in 1860–61, was succeeded by another American, Burgevine, and he by two Englishmen, Holland and Cooke. General Ward drilled the army and really raised it from a rabble into a disciplined and effective force. And though the foreign community regarded him as an adventurer, the Chinese looked up to him as an able leader and, after his death at Tsz'ki in 1861, erected a shrine to his memory before which incense was kept burning for many years, perhaps to this day. Gordon accepted his appointment in March, 1863, and with Li Hung Chang took command of the imperial forces. He improved upon the methods of General Ward; and within little more than a year, drilled and led by him, the Ever Victorious Army turned the tide of defeat and began to vindicate its vainglorious title. By a series of thirty-three battles, several of them brilliant and daring exploits, some of them carrying fortified cities by storm, some of them general actions in the field, the great Taiping Rebellion was suppressed. In China, as well as before Sebastopol

[4]Frederick T. Ward, of Salem, Mass.

and in the Soudan, the famous soldier exhibited not only great military genius but still more a generous devotion of self to the service of others. It did not win a Celestial shrine and smoking incense, but it is commemorated in the inscription recorded later on his monument at St. Paul's—"always ready to give his strength to the weak, his substance to the poor, his sympathy to the suffering, and his life to God."*

The adventures chronicled here in this chapter formed but one episode in this tremendous tragedy of the Taipings. For five months we were curious spectators of a Chinese war, and the scenes we witnessed left ineffaceable memories. We began with sympathy for the new cause. We ended with sympathy for the lacerated empire. A contest in which a Christian knight like Gordon could embark his conscience and his sword was worth waging, and is worth recording. Some of the battles we saw before he arrived were highly dramatic, and when they did not draw blood were spectacular and entertaining.

On the night of the sixth of September 1853, as the *Saratoga* was lying peacefully at anchor off

*For more information on Frederick T. Ward, whose foreign legion sponsored by Shanghi's merchants against the Taipings earned the sobriquet of "Ever Victorious Army"; Henry A. Burgevine, a thieving conspirator; and Charles George "Chinese" Gordon, a celebrated British officer and colonial administrator, see Dudden, *The American Pacific*, p. 116. Gordon again distinguished himself at Sebastopol in the Crimean War (1854) and died in the siege of Khartoum in the Sudan.—Ed.

Shanghai, a band of Canton and Fohkien assassins rose within the city, expelled the *taotai*, put some of his officials to the sword, sacked their houses, and seized the government. A reign of terror followed. For some days these Celestial Robespierres and Marats had their own bloody way. Everything that could get away fled. Junks scuttled off from the docks as fast as they could unmoor, until scarcely a sampan was left, and the riverfront was as bare as an abandoned canal. Multitudes left their homes and sought safety in flight. At last the conspirators fearing that the city would become literally depopulated, closed the gates and made desertion a capital crime.

Within a month the imperial forces assembled to retake the fallen city. They came trooping over the plains in straggling battalions, flocking in fleets up the river from the coast and down the streams from the interior. We visited their camps. It was a sight worth seeing. I would not speak disrespectfully of the "tigers" of China–a name often borne by the national troops, not on account of their man-eating propensities, nor for their bravery, but simply because they so frequently carried the brute's head painted on their shields. We found them a mongrel crowd, swarthy, boorish, lank, and much bedizened in their parti-colored uniforms. (Bear in mind that this was seven years before General Ward, a whole decade before Gordon.) Now and then a big trooper looked well-fed and unctuous. But the rank and file were tatterdemalions. In those faraway days, coming from the interior as they did, they had never seen a Westerner, and we were as great a curiosity to them as they were to us. They thronged around us, fingered our clothing and felt of our hands and faces. They unbuttoned our collars and inspected our necks. Nor would they be satisfied till we had bared our arms and bosoms to convince them that our pallid complexion was not a kind of wash that would rub off.

Their first summons to the insurgents only met with derision. And with stolid Mongolian patience, they set themselves down to the task of beleaguering the city. Their operations on the riverside were in plain view from our decks and we watched many a battle. Some were serious, some were comic. In their land skirmishes they commonly left their artillery at the camp, and equipped with spears, swords, knives, and jingals, they charged toward the walls brandishing their weapons, waving their flags, beating their gongs, blazing away with their jingals, hooting and scoffing at the enemy. They were met with similar tactics from the ramparts—gongs, shouts, banners, bravado, and guns, which last did the business and sent the assailants scampering back toward the camp. Rallied by their screaming leaders, they would get into line again and would repeat the maneuvers, with the same results. Sometimes the rebels sallied from the gates and chased their assailants off the ground, to be driven back in turn to the shelter of the walls. And so on for hours; the same ground would be fought over, or rather raced over, half a dozen times in a single fight. On both sides discretion seemed to be generally regarded as the better part of valor. Neither party betrayed any anxiety to get too near the other.

Each brave doubtless felt a wholesome respect for his own skin. The risks involved were too much like those referred to by Lord Chatham[5] when he was speaking of General Gage shut up in Boston: "His situation reminds me, my lords, of the answer of a French general in the civil wars of France–M. Condé opposed to M. Turenne. He was asked how it happened that he did not take his adversary prisoner, as he was often very near him. *'J'ai peur'*, replied Condé very honestly, *'J'ai peur qu'il ne me prenne!'* "[*]

In the early part of the siege there were some odd encounters in which the losses were by desertion. A storming party would advance brimful of fight. A parley ensues. Then as if inspired with sudden valor half the assailants rush to the walls, plant their scaling ladders, dash up the parapet, swarm on the ramparts, and drawing up their ladders after them fraternize with the rebels. The balance of the assaulting party gaze stupidly at the phenomenon and

[5]Speech on removing the troops from Boston, House of Lords, January 20, 1775.

[*]"I feared that he did not want capturing."–Ed.

then turn campward sadder and wiser men; somewhat hastened on the home stretch by a parting volley from their late comrades in arms.

To the Chinese the art of gunnery was then in its infancy. The handling of their batteries was skillfully awkward. To fire was the main thing, specially if it made the welkin roar; but how the piece was loaded and whither aimed did not appear to be matters of prime importance. The charge was loose powder, and that of a poor make. When a bombardment was prolonged until after dark, we frequently saw the powder burning and dropping into the river many rods away from the muzzle of the gun. And China had been using gunpowder in battle for four centuries, and in fireworks for a thousand years before that. One would think that in that length of time even slow-moving China might have learned to make it better; or that the powder might, if left to itself, have grown better by some process of evolution. In the attacks on the land side, instead of shot and shell, the missiles often consisted of a bucketful of slugs, nails, fragments of pottery, brick, old iron, pebble stones, and the like–a charge which would spread enough to sow an acre of ground.

The north gate of the city was a sort of tower or bastion, with an eighteen-pounder mounted in the embrasure above the portal. A few rods away stood two houses belonging to an American mission and occupied by two missionary families. The families had been removed at the outbreak of hostilities; but to keep the premises from being seized and garrisoned by either party as a convenient point from which to attack, the gentlemen were obliged to stay by and hold them under the protection of the flag. One of these teachers, though a southron and used to firearms, was of somewhat nervous temperament and did not enjoy his lonely vigils. He invited me to share them and I often did so. The enclosure stood in the center of the common field of action; and on two of those occasions we were roused from our slumbers by a midnight battle going on right around the house. If any of my readers have ever been present in a really serious Chinese shindy, they can easily imagine the hullabaloo; the infernal racket and din–the shouts, yells, screams–the discharge of jingals and fire-arrows–and every few moments the explosion of the big gun over the gate. It is not altogether playful to look out from your chamber window and see the midnight blackness lighted up by incessant flashes from muskets and jingals, or to trace by its comet tail of sparks the flight of a rocket fire-arrow, knowing, too, that every discharge may carry death to some miserable combatant. I have one of those fire-arrows beside me as I write, picked up on the field of battle; it is dumb now and has never confessed its murderous deeds. How much havoc the noisy gun on the bastion may have carried into the ranks of the assailants, I cannot say; but the miscellaneous charge peppered our house every time from foundation to ridgepole, and the next morning we picked out nails and slugs by the handful.

Among other tricks of the strategy, the besiegers attempted mining. On one occasion they found themselves on the eve of success. The workmen had burrowed through the soil until they were actually beneath the walls. The tidings flew to camp. Great preparations were made. A doughty column was ready to storm the breach, and mighty deeds were promised. Meanwhile the rebels were not idle. They had spies. And having located the approaching mine they had sunk a deep counter-trench at right angles and kept it filled with water. When forty miners reached it, the thin partition of clay burst with sudden roar. A brief struggle in the dark and all was over. That was the end of their experiments under ground.

I was threading the narrow streets one day toward the walls when I suddenly came upon a crowd. It was not so noisy as Chinese mobs often are. There was no laughter, and the chatter here and there was in a subdued undertone. They were watching something. I elbowed my way in and not being adept in the vernacular inquired by signs what was the matter. They pointed up at the side of a shop. There hung, suspended by its cue, a ghastly head. It was a young brave who had been caught and decapitated by the imperial "tigers." Poor wretch, the bruises and slashes on his pate showed how hard he had fought for life. But his dream of military glory had come to an untimely end. He was of no further use to his day and generation than to dangle his skull from a peg by the roadside as a warning to his fellow rebels. What honors his heroism may have won for him in the Chinese heaven I cannot say, not having yet traveled in those parts. Per adventure he may have rivaled the high reward bestowed on his countryman General Chin. That redoubtable warrior commanded the forts at the mouth of the Wusung in the Opium War of 1842 and there fell in battle. In recognition of his services his family was ennobled, his image was set up in Shanghai, and for many years incense was kept burning before it. But far beyond these trivial honors was the promotion he received above. According to a current rumor in Shanghai two or three weeks after his death, Chin sent down word that he had been elevated by the supreme ruler of heaven to the position of second general-in-chief to the Board of Thunder; so that though he could not exterminate the foreign devils while in the flesh, he could still give them an occasional shock from the clouds!

My path led me presently out into the open and across a paddy-field directly to the wall and the north gate. I was wandering along in a sobered mood when "bang" went the eighteen pounder on the bastion just before me. The gunners doubtless meant to aim at the imperialist camp about a mile off; but as they had loaded up with a generous overdose of slugs, nails, bits of glass, and rock, the charge spread like a fan and went screaming through the air, ripping off showers of leaves and twigs from the trees, plowing up the grass, and doing all sorts of execution except damaging or frightening the enemy. Some of the slugs struck and rebounded in the gravel at my feet; whereupon I shook my fist at the gun's crew and beat a masterly retreat, in good order and without loss of baggage or temper.

Coming back to the house of a young missionary whom I knew, I rang at the gate. He sent a coolie to admit me, but meanwhile called from the window, "Roll yourself up small–the balls are flying lively this morning." I went in and we gathered up his penates for flight. Several balls had riddled his house, smashing the crockery, puncturing the library, going through his books quicker and more thoroughly than he had ever done himself, and turning things generally into complete bric-a-brac. His family had been sent to the foreign quarter that morning; and, by putting together all the necessary traps, we presently fastened up the premises and quickly followed them.

There was a battle every two or three days. The land attacks were frequently seconded by the fleet on the river. It was interesting, and sometimes droll, to watch the evolutions of forty or fifty junks beating about on the tide and bombarding the fort at the east gate. The firing was irregular and incessant. The river was ploughed by the passing shot and well be-fountained with jets of spray. Occasional stray balls went over the fort into the city, but did little harm beyond frightening the dogs, splintering the tiles, and sending up a cloud of dust from a demolished roof.

The rebels had purchased a foreign barque and a brig, and these with three or four native gunboats they had heavily armed and equipped, and had moored them off the east gate battery. The imperialists then attacked them. After a furious duel with broadsides, two junks laid the two vessels alongside and boarded them. A desperate hand-to-hand fight on deck made short work of it. We could see the wretched crews leaping overboard in mortal terror and making for the shore. Not one lived to reach it. The victors jumped into their boats, dashed after them, and with clubs and spears dispatched them in the water.

One afternoon there was an unusual stir in the fleet. We were on the alert to watch developments. Presently a large flotilla of boats gathered from the various junks and pulled up by us gaily decked with banners and loaded to the gunwales with warriors intent on valorous deeds. They grinned at us as they passed, as if to assert a familiar brotherhood in arms and to claim our endorsement of the bloody job they had in hand. Their objective point was a small river battery near us—so near that we could see the faces of the combatants. Some of us younger sprigs of the navy, to get a better view of such an object lesson in actual warfare, scrambled like monkeys to the mizzentop and spent the balance of the afternoon taking in a bird's-eye view of the scene.

The rebels made a desperate stand and for a time the fighting was hot enough to satisfy Mars himself. Swords, jingals, spears, clubs pounded, punched, roared, and flashed on both sides. The rebels broke. Some dropped and died where they fought. Some fled, and their streaming wounds printed their tracks on the pavement in red. The victors turned the captured battery on the fugitives. How many were mowed down as the fatal shot ploughed those crowded streets we never knew. They must have been consumed in the flames where they fell, for the troops fired the houses in order to burn out the suburbs, and whole streets melted away before our eyes. We could see the forlorn inhabitants snatching whatever they could save and rushing in a maddened stream for the foreign quarter; some loaded with the contents of their shops, some with the tools of their trade, some with pots, pans, baskets, tables on their heads and children in their arms, some with their old mothers on their backs. The wind blew fresh and fanned the flames, and the whole district looked like the crater of a volcano. All that afternoon and into night and all the next day the fires went roaring like a furnace and devouring whatever was left to burn. When they stopped for lack of more worlds to conquer, there lay spread before us the ashes of temples, dwellings, tea gardens, hongs, godowns, and shops—two square miles swept level with the ground—a dismal holocaust to the god of war.

A few days later the whole fleet got underway. That east gate battery had not been silenced. Something must be done. All the afternoon the whole rabble of forty or fifty junks were beating to and fro off the battery and pounding away with boisterous and imbecile fire. We youngsters watched it as usual from the mizzentop. The admiral seemed easily satisfied with the glory and noise he had achieved, and very likely was hungry for his supper, for by five o'clock he signaled the fleet back to the anchorage. But two junks panted for more. Breaking from the line they dashed across the river and beached themselves directly under the ramparts, determined to carry the fort or die in the attempt. It was brilliant and brave; but in the expressive rhetoric of the shops, "too much no can!" The rebels were literally too many for them. Murderous volleys poured from guns little and big, and blazing fireballs came crashing down upon their decks, until the successive explosions appeared like one continuous flash. Both vessels were soon engulfed in flames. Their gallant crews driven from their guns fought like wild beasts. In the midst of the bloody struggle the fire reached the magazines and, with a frightful explosion, both vessels went thundering into the sky. An instant hush silenced every gun. An enormous white sulfurous cloud rose majestically and spread umbrella-like over the scene, and out of its folds came dropping big guns, blazing sails and spars, and fragments of men. The numbers destroyed on the two junks may not have exceeded the list of those who so suddenly went to their death on our ill-starred *Maine** at Havana; but in this duel on the Wusung not a soul survived to tell the tale.

A few days after, in a lucid interval between the battles, some of us strolled up there to view the remains. It was no light task to pick our way through the burnt district, where the streets were obliterated and ragged piles of ruin faced us wherever we turned. By tacking and wearing toward every point of the compass we at last zigzagged our way to the spot. There lay the blackened hulls, or rather the undershells of them. All the upper works were gone, clean scooped out by the force of the explosion. Our friends the enemy were greatly flattered by our interest in their prowess and issuing from the fort gathered round and overwhelmed us with voluble attentions. Not only that, but they took us within their fortress and showed us its strong defenses. Where upon we made yet another very interesting

*U.S.S. *Maine*, on February 15, 1898, blew up in Havana harbor in an explosion that killed 260 officers and men. The incident helped to precipitate the Spanish-American War.—Ed.

discovery. There was the table-boy of our port steerage mess installed in the fort as a high official in silks and buttons. He had skipped some weeks before. And what better qualification could be desired for a captaincy in the rebel artillery than that he had served on an American man-of-war? He saw that we recognized him; but his value as a servant had not been so priceless nor his loss so irreparable that we cared to disturb his dreams of military fame.

In February 1854, we were summoned away from these lively scenes to attend to what a Celestial would call "pidgin" of our own. There followed the second chapter in the story of the Japan expedition and signing of the treaty. The *Plymouth* took our place at Shanghai, and the *Saratoga*, bearing the new treaty, spread her white wings for home. And while our rusty old seabird was flying, rolling, plunging homeward round the Horn as fast as its canvas and tempest could drive her, events went tripping on almost as nimbly in the land of the yellow dragon. The *Plymouth* found plenty of interesting things to watch.[6]

Matters had not been running smoothly between the Celestials and their foreign neighbors. An un-

[6]On account of our *alibi,* the adventures contained in the rest of this chapter I cannot record as an eyewitness. But fortunately I have a letter from a friend who happened to visit Shanghai in a merchantman soon after we left, and who saw and shared in the events. I find some assistance also in incidental allusions from various travelers of the day.

expected stroke of idiocy on the part of the Chinese commander brought affairs to a focus. An American merchant on his way to his place of business in his own private boat, over which the American flag was flying, was hailed by one of the war junks and ordered alongside. He paid no attention to the order and kept on his way. A second and more peremptory hail was accompanied by a shot, and he pulled to the junk to demand the cause of the outrage. He was seized and made prisoner, his flag torn to shreds and trampled underfoot.

When the affair was reported to the commander of the *Plymouth* an officer was instantly sent with a boat's crew who rescued him. But the insult to the flag was a graver matter. After consultation with the American consul, Commander Kelly sent notice to the Chinese chief and to the authorities of the city that on the following Monday at one o'clock the fleet should as an atonement publicly salute the American flag, or he would blow every junk out of the water. Monday morn he got underway, moved down and dropped anchor in the circle of junks with ports open, guns trained, and men at quarters; and at the appointed moment the Stars and Stripes rose to the masthead of the admiral's flagship and was humbly saluted with Chinese powder. One refractory junk started to escape, but a ball from the *Plymouth* crashed through her ribs and brought her round into line. As an additional lesson some of the junks were then dismantled, their guns were spiked, and their small arms were also thrown overboard.

These irregular conflicts made it manifest that it was to the common interest of both foreigners and natives to emancipate the stricken city and turn the pirates out. The Imps too (as the rebels called them with a pardonable abbreviation of the foreign term) had become an unbearable nuisance, and the downfall of the city would bring things to an end. Their departure would be hailed with applause. It was neither English nor Americans however who brought matters at last to a crisis. The nearest foreign suburb to the native city happened to be the French, which lay on the north side and bordered on the moat. The situation came past endurance; the French decided to join the Imps in a combined assault. The attempt was made January 6, 1855, and proved a failure. Another a month later produced a like result. A year of fighting had given the rebels fine practice and they had profited by it. But though not dislodged they were alarmed, and concluding that other such assaults might make the place too hot for them, decamped in the night of February sixteenth. Like the rest of their compatriots they left mementos of their departure in bloody and smoking ruins.

This ended the Taiping tragedy in Shanghai. Five years later another rebel army marched on the city, ravaging and plundering the country as it advanced; but the French and English had armed to protect their homes, and joining the Imperialists, inflicted upon the invaders a bloody repulse. Another invasion was ordered by the Taiping-wang in 1862; and it was the menacing operations of this filibustering force that finally led to the appointment of Chinese Gordon as the leader of the Ever Victorious Army in 1863. The result is well-known to the world.

It is not surprising that the great insurrection should have been hailed at first as the advent of a national deliverance. The Chinese themselves, those who cared enough about their country to give it any thought, hoped that it might emancipate them from their Manchu conquerors and reinstate the native dynasty on the throne. Foreigners, in so far as they expected anything serious, hoped that it might result in the further opening of the reluctant empire to Western civilization and Western trade. Both were doomed to disappointment. What had seemed to rise as a golden dawn soon darkened, and finally closed in a night of terror, like one of their own frightful typhoons. And when the Heavenly King took his own life while in his Nanking palace, the curtain fell not on the pathetic failure of a people's struggle for freedom, but on the fortunate collapse of a tragedy which had nothing left for motive but vengeance and pillage and lust. With that final blow the empire was released from the toils of a fiery conflict that was rending her heart and life. Peace proclaimed itself in the usual flourishes of Chinese rhetoric, and the busy myriads settled down to the industries that constitute their life and that hold the great loose-jointed country together.

With all her faults there is something about the big empire that wins the visitor who treads her shores. Those who know the Chinese best come to like them most. Their peculiarities we can smile at and condone. They can do the same with ours. One must admit that the character of the Chinese is a medley of contradictions: honest and industrious, practical, shrewd, patient, docile, good-natured, yet capable of frenzied outbursts of cruelty. And yet the bankers and merchants are men of probity whose word is as good as their bond, phlegmatic, unemotional, unimaginative, conservative, and superstitious, with a national vanity the most egregious and a civil service the most corrupt on the globe, content with things as they are and incapable of initiative. There is in the average Chinaman a certain sturdiness and steadiness of temperament, a common sense, a genius for industry and honesty. He is not poetic but practical, not transcendental and speculative but persistent and plodding. It makes one's blood boil to think of the unpatriotism and the blundering medieval mismanagement that made such a mammoth of an empire and swarming with such practical matter-of-fact people let itself be whipped by little Japan. But the defeat carried with it a prodigious lesson, which China has slowly set herself to learn. The two peoples are widely different. If the Japanese might conceivably be compounded by melting together a Frenchman and a Greek, with a dash of Arab, to make the Chinaman one needs only Tartar and Teuton. If the Celestial may not be so brilliant as the Japanese, neither is he so nervous and fickle. He may be slow, but he is virile, has stuff in him, and equilibrium. China has great capacity for the practical arts, and long before the Sunrise Kingdom had been heard of in the West she had bestowed on the world such priceless commodities as silk, paper, tea, gunpowder, and the compass. No one who really loves China can listen with patience to the schemes of Western avarice, or think calmly of this proud antique ever being in danger of vivisection into "spheres of influence." If the powers leave the empire in her integrity, as agreed upon by the two great antagonists, Russia and Japan, in their treaty of peace just now completed, it is safe to predict that the future will show an "open door" much wider open than ever before to the best influences of the West.

IX

The Expedition Again and the Opening of Japan

IN FEBRUARY 1854, the American fleet again met in Yedo Bay. It went the first time with four ships, the second time with nine. The Western barbarian had come to get his answer. Instead of stopping at Uraga as he had done the year before, Commodore Perry moved up to Kanagawa, where the city of Yokohama now stands, some twenty-five miles above Uraga and within ten or fifteen miles of Yedo. So powerful a force within an hour's sail of their great metropolis must have expedited the negotiations. And though the American demands were contested inch by inch, yet it was done with good nature and the commissioners almost invariably yielded.

Here enters another actor. As in all historical movements, and certainly in all novels, other influences were at work behind the scenes. It was only another part of the mystery brooding over this strange land that forces unknown and unsuspected should be working for us in the dark. Not until years after did it transpire what a friend we had in Nakahama Manjiro, a Japanese waif, whose story reads like a romance. In 1838, he was out fishing with two other boys when their boat was caught in the current, carried out to sea, and wrecked on a desolate island. There for half a year, they lived a Robinson Crusoe life until picked off the island by an American whaling ship and brought to Honolulu where Nakahama learned the language of his new friends. Finally coming to the United States, he received an education. Another whaling voyage, a visit to the California mines, and he was back in Honolulu anxious to revisit his native land. Nothing could deter him. The dissuasions of his friends, the distance and perils of the way, the likelihood of being beheaded for his pains if he should succeed—no argument or obstacle could stand for a moment before his unutterable longing for home.

In due time, therefore, Nakahama and his two comrades, now grown from lads to young men of twenty-five, were equipped with a whaleboat, a sack of ship's biscuit, a *Bowditch's Navigator** and a compass, and were put on board an American merchantman bound to Shanghai. A few miles from Lew Chew, they and their whaleboat were launched and committed to the waves. After a hard day's pull, they reached the shore, only to be arrested and imprisoned; six months later they were forwarded in a trading junk to Japan, to be imprisoned again, this time for three years. It would seem that

*Nathaniel Bowditch (1773–1838), American navigator and mathematician, who, under his own name, published *The American Practical Navigator* (1802–19); it has been published since 1867 by the United States Hydrographic Office.—Ed.

Japanese Woman at Shimoda; from
The Expedition of an American Squadron

Japanese Cooper; from
The Expedition of an American Squadron

Illustrations Courtesy University of Chicago Library

for three whole years, the officials wrestled with the problem before they could decide whether getting blown off the coast in boyhood and being brought back in manhood constituted a capital crime. The year 1853 came round. The Perry expedition had come and gone, and was to come again. Here was a captive in their dungeons who had actually lived in the country of these Western barbarians, spoke their uncouth language, and knew their crafty ways. Why behead an expert just when he was needed? Instead they brought him to court and made him open his budget of information. From a prisoner he was transformed into a noble and decorated with the two swords. By order of government he was provided with a crew of carpenters and required to build a whole fleet of whaleboats like his own; and then, with a corps of scribes, he was directed to translate his *Bowditch's Navigator* and make a score of copies for the use of the Japanese marine. One of these copies Nakahama afterwards gave to his friend Chaplain Damon in Honolulu, and it was on exhibition at the Centennial Exposition in Philadelphia in 1876. Dr. Damon had often inquired after the three adventurers but had never learned their fate.

One morning, years after the treaty had been signed, a Japanese ship anchored off Honolulu and her commander came on shore to call on our Dr. Damon. It was no other than long-lost Nakahama, who was now an officer in the Japanese navy. The mutual explanations can be imagined. "Where were you at the time of the expedition?" asked the chaplain. "I was in a room adjoining that in which the negotiations were going on," said Nakahama. "I was not allowed to see or communicate with any of the Americans. But each document from Commodore Perry I translated before it was handed to the commissioners, and the replies also I translated into English before they went to the commodore." Which explains what so mystified our diplomats at the time—that the papers from the "party of the second part" came to them not alone in Dutch and Japanese but in English also. Nakahama was more than interpreter. He knew the American people, the magnitude of their country, their wealth and commerce, their prestige and power. He believed in them. He was the channel through which by a kind of preordination American ideas filtered into Japan. It is easy to recognize the divine preparation of the man, an overruling plan and purpose in his whole training from the hour when the three castaways drifted to sea in an open boat until the day when the Sunrise Kingdom faced the demands of the American fleet.

Meanwhile the stern public sentiment of this isolated nation was rapidly melting away before our neighborly advances. The people seemed to be glad of our coming. They flocked on board and were received as friends. They admired our ships. They liked our dinners. As an impartial historian I

Japanese Soldiers at Yokohama; from The Expedition of an American Squadron

Courtesy The Beverly R. Robinson Collection, United States Naval Academy Museum, Annapolis, Maryland

must admit that they took kindly, sometimes convivially, to our brandies and wines. And on shore these courtesies were duly reciprocated. The negotiations took time. Many meetings were held; on most of these occasions, an entertainment was served by the Japanese in native style. Sidney Smith once said of his countrymen that "an Englishman is like an oyster–you must get into him with a knife and fork." That was one of the ways we got into the country of Japan; many a treat went into that treaty.

At one of these dainty banquets, it was my good fortune to be one of the guests. It was the day when the Mikado's gifts to our government were exhibited. They were samples of both the fine arts and the mechanical arts of the country; some of them exquisitely graceful, some showing rather the ingenuity and skill of plain handicraft. The cabinet lacquer-work especially surpassed in artistic design and beauty of finish anything of the kind we had seen. The other presents were silks, crapes, silverware, bronzes, porcelains, furniture, and samples of household utensils and artisans' tools. For some years after the return of the fleet, these gifts could be seen at the Patent Office. I believe they are now exhibited in the National Museum at Washington.

When we had sufficiently admired all the pretty things, our genial hosts led us to the banquet room, and dinner was set on. This was, of course, composed of native viands, served in native style, and to be eaten with native chopsticks. To eat in that method requires either long practice or that the applicant be to the manner born. If you are a Western barbarian and have not had the advantage of oriental training, do not attempt it, at least when you are hungry; the results are apt to be disappointing. The dinner was most abundant. To our Saxon sea appetites, it was toothsome; and what with chopsticks and our own fingers and penknives, we wrestled with it in masterly fashion. First they seated us on benches in long rows around the hall and then ranged similar benches before us spread with scarlet tea-cloths. Upon these in front of each guest was set a small wooden lacquered stand six or eight inches high and twelve or fifteen square, protected by a rim that kept the dainty dishes from crowding each other off. Mine was filled with the most delicate porcelains, and, albeit somewhat hungry, I longed to appropriate the ceramics instead of the provender. The menu had its unique points; there were soups, vegetables, oysters, crabs, boiled eggs, pickled fish, seaweed jelly, and other compounds that we did not quite recognize and, therefore, felt toward them that hesitating awe experienced by the elder Mr. Weller in the presence of "weal pie."* The drinks were tea, served as always in the East without alloy of sugar or cream, and *saki*, a strong colorless alcohol distilled from

*A metaphoric reference by Sewall to Charles Dickens's unforgettable characterization of the elder Samuel Weller in *The Pickwick Papers*.—Ed.

Dinner Given to the Japanese Commissioners on Board U.S.S. Powhatan; *from* The Expedition of an American Squadron

Courtesy University of Chicago Library

rice, somewhat like the *samshu* or "white wine" of China. To these edibles and potables we applied ourselves with courage, and, considering our disabilities with the chopsticks, they proved remarkably evanescent. More *saki* and tea prepared us for a dessert of candied nuts, sponge cake, cookies of various genera and species, sugared fruit, and confectionery. When all was done, our hosts brought us each a sheet of bamboo paper to wrap up and carry away what we had not consumed. Some of mine were still extant when I reached home seven months later.

This was a small point of etiquette they observed themselves, and it led sometimes to interesting results. One day at a dinner party on board the flagship, a Japanese functionary fell in love with a frosted cake and a bottle of hock. According to custom, he desired to take them home. But it was late, and his potations having made him too unsteady to be the bearer of any other freight, the commodore promised to send them by a special messenger in the morning. Morning came, but not the cake. During the night that had absconded; some unregenerate tar had stowed it away for safekeeping. Here was a terrible dilemma. What if the negotiations should be imperiled for lack of that cake! A sort of coroner's inquest was hastily summoned to sit on the missing loaf. The verdict was, "Send the hock, but tell him that, in America, we present cake in the evening." The guest was entirely satisfied, and, by sunset, another frosted cake like the stolen one was concocted at the galley and was then duly sent on shore.

After the dinner our hosts conducted us to the beach. Among the presents was a large supply of rice for the fleet. It was put up in straw sacks or bales containing about 125 pounds each. By the pile stood a company of athletes and gymnasts chosen from the peasantry for their strength and size and trained for the service and entertainment of the court. At a signal from their leader, who was himself a giant of muscle and fat, a sort of human Jumbo, they began transporting the rice to the boats. It was more frolic than work. Some of them bore a bale on each hand above their heads, some would carry two laid crosswise on the shoulders and head, while others performed dexterous feats of tossing, catching, balancing them, or turning somersaults with them. I saw one nimble Titan fasten his talons in a sack, throw it down on the sand still keeping his hold, turn a somersault over it, throw it over him as he revolved, and come down sitting on the beach with the sack in his lap. Beat that who can. If you imagine it "as easy as preaching," try it the next time in a gymnasium. But let me advise you, first make your will.

Later in the afternoon, the same athletes entertained us with a wrestling match. A ring had been prepared in the area of the council house and the ground softened by the spade. Enter twenty-five

Wrestlers at Yokohama; from The Expedition of an American Squadron

Courtesy The Beverly R. Robinson Collection, United States Naval Academy Museum, Annapolis, Maryland

performers in a slow and dignified procession, stripped to the loincloth, and equipped with satin aprons gorgeously embroidered and fringed. Ranging themselves in a circle around the ring, with grave pomp they enacted a series of incantations and passes. Then they filed off to the rear and laid aside their satin millinery for business. As their names were called by the master of ceremonies, a pair of them would advance, take their stand at opposite points of the ring, crouch on their heels, and repeat the mysterious passes. Then, entering the circle and warily approaching each other, they again crouched, again gesticulated, and finally, with a demoniac yell, sprang at each other like two monstrous billygoats. They used the head, not the fist. They plunged into each other, capered wildly about, and dove into each other headlong, butted each other on the breast and shoulders with frantic violence. Some of them, I noticed, had raised large welts on their foreheads by frequent indulgence in this frisky pastime, and some of them were dripping with the blood that oozed from the fat creases of their necks. An hour sufficed for these huge calisthenics. When it was all over and the puffing giants had collapsed, the ring smoked with the dust of battle and looked as if it had been trampled and torn by a herd of gamboling elephants.

Another spectacle that afternoon, more prophetic of the new future just opening on the empire, was the first railroading in Japan. Among the presents to the Mikado, we carried a railroad; not, to be sure, a fully equipped road, well weighted with mortgage bonds and watered stock, tied up in a merger or run by a receiver; but so much of the genuine article as is represented by the rails, the engine, and a car. In the rear of the council house, the mechanics of the squadron had laid the circular track, and thither our gentle hosts now led us. There stood the locomotive and car, exquisite specimens of American workmanship, the engine already hissing and fuming, impatient to show itself off, the car as sumptuous as the richest woods and the finest art could make it. The whole was constructed on a scale of one-quarter size, and so nothing larger than a St. Bernard dog or a French doll could enter the dainty rosewood door. The engineer sat on the tender and bestowed his legs along the engine. And when a timid Japanese was finally induced to take a John Gilpin ride, he had to sit on the roof of the car and stow his feet on the tender. You can imagine with what a death grip he clung to the eaves of the car, and how his teeth chattered and his robes fluttered as he flashed around the circle. He thought he was a deadhead; and so indeed he was. This miniature railroad was for some years kept as a sort of imperial toy. A storehouse was built for its safekeeping; every little while, they would relay the track and gay parties of princes and courtiers would go flying around on a sort of circular picnic. The empire has long since outgrown

Delivering of the American "Presents" at Yokohama; from The Expedition of an American Squadron

Courtesy University of Chicago Library

the toy and is laying its own railroads in all directions. Every year witnesses substantial additions to the mileage, the travel, and the traffic.

The telegraph seemed to be more of a puzzle to them than the steam engine. We carried them a line fifteen miles long and set up a short stretch of it as a sample. They would go to one end, deliver a message, and then trot mystified to the other end, only to find their message safely arrived, written out, and waiting for them. It was just Yankee magic, necromancy, witchcraft! But they have long since become adept in the same magic, and their picturesque land is interlacing itself all over with an ever expanding web of wires.

Another of our presents was a brass Dahlgren howitzer.* Not long after, a thousand pieces like it had been cast at their foundries and were mounted in their forts. It was from these guns that their salutes on Washington's birthday and the Fourth of July were appropriately fired. Washington's name and fame had reached the empire long before the expedition had been dreamed of; "a very great man," they said, "we know him very well in Japan."

After many meetings, the negotiations finally were completed and the treaty signed on Friday, the thirty-first day of March 1854. Our ship had been longest in commission of the whole squadron

*John Adolphus Bernard Dahlgren (1809–70), American naval officer, an ordinance expert, the designer of the nine-inch and eleven-inch guns that were called the Dahlgrens.—Ed.

and was, therefore, selected to bring the precious document away; and having received the bearer of dispatches, Captain H. A. Adams, on the fourth of April, the *Saratoga* spread her white wings for home. It was inspiring and to us who were at last homeward bound, it was thrilling to hear the rousing cheers from each ship as we passed down the line, and, from the commodore's band, the strains of "Home, Sweet Home." We were soon out on the Pacific again, and that was our good-bye to the fleet and to Japan. At Honolulu, Captain Adams left us for Panama and reached Washington with the treaty sometime in June. The *Saratoga*, wishing in vain for a Panama Canal to give her a short cut home, had yet to plough through boundless latitudes and longitudes. Calling at Tahiti, we lay for a week within the dreamy shadows of the verdure-clad hills that look down on the harbor of Papiete; then rolled and pitched and foamed along through the darkness and tempests and cold of Cape Horn, which we passed on the middle day of winter, July fifteenth; and after calling at Pernambuco, a port in Brazil, we finally dropped anchor at Charlestown Navy Yard in September, more than five months from Japan, and absent from America for four years. . . .

[We have omitted the rest of Chapter IX and all of Chapter X from the original *Logbook* because they do not further elaborate on the story of the opening of Japan.]

EDITOR'S EPILOGUE

And there came,
Breaking through the mist,
Roaring through the sea,
Four black dragons,
Spitting fire.[1]

JOHN SMITH SEWALL died in 1911, sixty-one years after he enlisted in the United States Navy. The Emperor Meiji died one year later, in 1912, long after Perry's historic expedition with Sewall aboard had opened up Japan to the world outside. In the Emperor Meiji's name, Japan modernized Japanese society virtually overnight, to leave behind forever, floating alone in the mists, the insular world of the shogunate, feudal and willfully isolated, in the middle of the sea.

Commodore Matthew Calbraith Perry had died a hero, in 1858, less than four years after his return from Japan. Gloriously, from an observant sailor's viewpoint, Sewall's *Logbook of the Captain's Clerk* illuminates Perry's extraordinary achievement. During his two voyages to the Bay of Edo, Perry firmly rejected the degrading harassments of the Japanese guard boats, which always surrounded all foreign vessels, as if they were actually under

[1]John Weidman and Stephen Sondheim, *Pacific Overtures*, a musical (New York: Theatre Communications Group, 1976, 1977, 1986, and 1991), p. 15.

arrest while in Japan's waters. Perry further made clear his intentions to treat with no Japanese emissary of a rank inferior to the highest officers of the Empire, and to win a reception in every detail honorable to himself and the country he represented. His hydrographic surveys conducted under the very guns of their defensive batteries demonstrated to the Japanese the futility of attempting to frighten away the Americans. And conscious that he was confronting a ceremonious people, Perry, by form and etiquette, invariably upheld the dignity of his mission. Hence, in the matter of gifts, the Commodore insured that presents should be exchanged merely as friendly courtesies, and he never accepted anything without returning at least its equivalent.

In his efforts to display the just power and technological superiority of the United States to the Japanese, Commodore Perry diligently sought to present the friendliest possible disposition to them that they might perceive the United States as desirous solely of a kindly relationship. On the one hand, he could respectfully demand a protection for American citizens who might find themselves in Japanese hands, while, on the other, courteously request a mutual cultivation of trade and commerce. He reminded the Japanese how closely in physical terms their islands had been brought to the United States by the nation's expansion to the Pacific Coast, the admission of the State of California, and

John Smith Sewall, about the time he wrote Logbook

Courtesy Bowdoin College, Brunswick, Maine

the development of a steam-powered navy. How well he succeeded is now visible in Shimoda, the site of the first United States Consulate in Japan. Visitors will find to this day a bust of Matthew Perry facing the harbor, an *Opening of Japan* monument inscribed with Perry's conciliatory words, and numerous other testimonials and symbols of Japanese-American friendship.

On leaving the navy, John Smith Sewall returned to his home state of Maine. He took his Master of Arts degree at Bowdoin College in 1855, then graduated from Bangor Theological Seminary, in 1858, the year his commodore died. Ordained a Congregationalist minister in 1859, he served as a church pastor, 1859–67, in Wenham, Massachusetts. Back at Bowdoin again, he taught this time as Professor of Homiletics (the art of preaching) and English Literature, 1867–75, before retiring as Professor of Homiletics and Sociology from Bangor Theological Seminary, his other *alma mater*, where he taught from 1875 to 1903. Of Japan's progress he exalted, as any evangelist might, over the optimistic tidings now reaching him from American missionaries who were proselytizing the Christian Gospel. Wrote Sewall: "The great island kingdom of the Orient is even now in the golden dawn of her renewal; and, now more than ever, in her physical beauty, her material expansion, her spiritual quickening, and the high place among the nations she has won by her arms and her generous diplomacy,

[Japan] deserves to wear the diadem of the ancient title, the Empire of the Rising Sun."[2]

The Commodore, the Captain's Clerk, and the Emperor of Japan–what chapters of history they wrote! Matthew Calbraith Perry died in 1858, John Smith Sewall died in 1911, and the Emperor Meiji died in 1912, the year that China's republic was born. Neither Asia nor America would ever be the same again.

A. P. D.

[2]Sewall, original *Logbook,* p. 231.

Index

INDEX

List of The Lakeside Classics

The Lakeside Classics

Number	Title	Year
1.	The Autobiography of Benjamin Franklin . . .	1903
2.	Inaugural Addresses of the Presidents of the United States from Washington to Lincoln . .	1904
3.	Inaugural Addresses of the Presidents of the United States from A. Johnson to T. Roosevelt .	1905
4.	Fruits of Solitude by William Penn	1906
5.	Memorable American Speeches I. The Colonial Period	1907
6.	Memorable American Speeches II. Democracy and Nationality	1908
7.	Memorable American Speeches III. Slavery	1909
8.	Memorable American Speeches IV. Secession, War, Reconstruction	1910
9.	The Autobiography of Gurdon Saltonstall Hubbard	1911
10.	Reminiscences of Early Chicago.	1912
11.	Reminiscences of Chicago During the Forties and Fifties	1913
12.	Reminiscences of Chicago During the Civil War .	1914
13.	Reminiscences of Chicago During the Great Fire .	1915
14.	Life of Black Hawk	1916
15.	The Indian Captivity of O. M. Spencer . . .	1917
16.	Pictures of Illinois One Hundred Years Ago . .	1918
17.	A Woman's Story of Pioneer Illinois by Christiana Holmes Tillson	1919
18.	The Conquest of the Illinois by George Rogers Clark	1920

Number	*Title*	*Year*
40.	The Early Day of Rock Island and Davenport by J. W. Spencer and J. M. D. Burrows	1942
41.	Six Years with the Texas Rangers by James B. Gillett	1943
42.	Growing Up with Southern Illinois by Daniel Harmon Brush	1944
43.	A History of Illinois, I, by Gov. Thomas Ford	1945
44.	A History of Illinois, II, by Gov. Thomas Ford	1946
45.	The Western Country in the 17th Century by Lamothe Cadillac and Pierre Liette	1947
46.	Across the Plains in Forty-nine by Reuben Cole Shaw	1948
47.	Pictures of Gold Rush California	1949
48.	Absaraka, Home of the Crows by Mrs. Margaret I. Carrington	1950
49.	The Truth about Geronimo by Britton Davis	1951
50.	My Life on the Plains by General George A. Custer	1952
51.	Three Years Among the Indians and Mexicans by General Thomas James	1953
52.	A Voyage to the Northwest Coast of America by Gabriel Franchère	1954
53.	War-Path and Bivouac by John F. Finerty	1955
54.	Milford's Memoir by Louis Leclerc de Milford	1956
55.	Uncle Dick Wootton by Howard Louis Conard	1957
56.	The Siege of Detroit in 1763	1958
57.	Among the Indians by Henry A. Boller	1959
58.	Hardtack and Coffee by John D. Billings	1960
59.	Outlines from the Outpost by John Esten Cooke	1961
60.	Colorado Volunteers in New Mexico, 1862 by Ovando J. Hollister	1962

Number	*Title*	*Year*
61.	Private Smith's Journal	1963
62.	Two Views of Gettysburg by Sir A. J. L. Fremantle and Frank Haskell	1964
63.	Dakota War Whoop by Harriet E. Bishop McConkey	1965
64.	Honolulu by Laura Fish Judd	1966
65.	Three Years in the Klondike by Jeremiah Lynch	1967
66.	Two Years' Residence on the English Prairie of Illinois by John Woods	1968
67.	John D. Young and the Colorado Gold Rush	1969
68.	My Experiences in the West by John S. Collins	1970
69.	Narratives of Colonial America, 1704-1765	1971
70.	Pioneers by Noah Harris Letts and Thomas Allen Banning, 1825-1865	1972
71.	Excursion Through America by Nicolaus Mohr	1973
72.	A Frenchman in Lincoln's America, Volume I, by Ernest Duvergier de Hauranne	1974
73.	A Frenchman in Lincoln's America, Volume II, by Ernest Duvergier de Hauranne	1975
74.	Narratives of the American Revolution	1976
75.	Advocates and Adversaries by Robert R. Rose	1977
76.	Hell among the Yearlings by Edmund Randolph	1978
77.	A Frontier Doctor by Henry F. Hoyt	1979
78.	Mrs. Hill's Journal – Civil War Reminiscences by Sarah Jane Full Hill	1980
79.	Skyward by Rear Admiral Richard E. Byrd	1981
80.	Helldorado by William M. Breakenridge	1982
81.	Mark Twain's West	1983
82.	Frontier Fighter by George W. Coe	1984
83.	Buckskin and Blanket Days by Thomas Henry Tibbles	1985

Number	*Title*	*Year*
84.	Autobiography of an English Soldier in the United States Army by George Ballentine	1986
85.	Life of Tom Horn	1987
86.	Children of Ol' Man River by Billy Bryant	1988
87.	Westward Journeys by Jesse A. Applegate and Lavinia Honeyman Porter	1989
88.	Narrative of My Captivity among the Sioux Indians by Fanny Kelly	1990
89.	We Pointed Them North by E. C. "Teddy Blue" Abbott and Helena Huntington Smith	1991
90.	A Texas Ranger by N. A. Jennings	1992
91.	From Mexican Days to the Gold Rush by James W. Marshall and E. Gould Buffum	1993
92.	My Life East and West by William S. Hart	1994
93.	The Logbook of the Captain's Clerk by John S. Sewall	1995

Designed, typeset, printed, and bound by
R.R. Donnelley & Sons Company.
Text was set in Bulmer typeface
using state-of-the-art composition
and page makeup software.
Text and images were electronically transferred
between manufacturing facilities.
Computer-to-plate technology was used to
convert electronic information into plates,
eliminating the film stage in print production.
The book was printed on 50-pound
White Lakeside Classics Opaque paper,
a 50-percent recycled sheet
manufactured by Glatfelter.
Cloth for the one-piece casebinding is
Roxite C Vellum Chocolate Brown,
manufactured by Holliston Mills Inc.